Explore
Your
Faith

Ed Strauss

BARBOUR
PUBLISHING

ISBN 978-1-61626-664-6

Published by Barbour Publishing, Inc., P.O. Box 719, Uhrichsville, Ohio 44683, www.barbourbooks.com

Our mission is to publish and distribute inspirational products offering exceptional value and biblical encouragement to the masses.

ECPA Member of the
Evangelical Christian
Publishers Association

Printed in the United States of America.

CONTENTS

1.

How Can I Be Sure That God Exists?

Through everything God made, they can clearly see his
invisible qualities—his eternal power and divine nature.
So they have no excuse for not knowing God.
ROMANS 1:20 NLT

Many agnostics feel that there's no way to be *sure* that God exists. They argue that one can *think* God exists and even be *convinced* that God exists, but at best skeptics argue that belief in God is a blind, illogical leap into the dark. But Christianity, as Paul explained to the Roman governor Festus, is a very reasonable faith. When Festus exclaimed, "You are out of your mind!" Paul replied, "I am not insane. . . . What I am saying is true and reasonable" (Acts 26:25 NIV).

It is reasonable because there is evidence. God created humankind and "never left them without evidence of himself" (Acts 14:17 NLT). What is the evidence? The amazing, complex world all around us and the universe above us. As Paul explained, the seasonal water cycles, the fertility of the earth, and the mystery of life itself are not only proof of God's existence, but also of His loving care. Modern biological sciences—particularly when one descends to the level of microbiology—confirm how breathtaking life is. The fingerprints of God are all over the plethora of earth's life forms. Their unique, complex, and interdependent designs are evidence that an intelligent designer made them.

David also tells us, "The heavens proclaim the glory of God. The skies display his craftsmanship" (Psalm 19:1 NLT). We now know the heavens to be far more awesome and astonishing than the ancients could possibly have imagined. Not only are the stars awe-inspiring and beautiful, but the universe—filled with galaxies, nebulae, red dwarfs, planets, moons, and black holes, not to mention the constant array of *new* discoveries—astounds us. More amazing still are the unseen laws of physics that govern everything, hold the visible universe together, and make it all work. It is an unparalleled masterpiece, and behind it is the Master Craftsman.

DISCUSSION QUESTIONS

1. Do you agree that Christianity is a "reasonable" faith?
2. Have you read books on intelligent design? Were they helpful?
3. What recent scientific discovery has amazed you?
4. What, to you, is the greatest natural evidence of God's existence?

2.

WHERE DID GOD COME FROM?

*Before. . .You had formed the earth and the world,
even from everlasting to everlasting, You are God.*
PSALM 90:2 NKJV

God has always existed. There has never been a time when God didn't exist. Since He has always been around, He didn't need to "come from" anywhere. Neither did He emerge from some other dimension into our present space-time reality. After all, God was the one who *created* space and time and all the dimensions in the first place.

One of God's titles is "the Eternal God" (Genesis 21:33 NIV). David, inspired by the Holy Spirit, stated, "You are from all eternity" (Psalm 93:2 NIV). The concept of infinity is difficult for our finite minds to grasp. In our experience, all life has both a beginning and an ending. Even the universe itself, as ancient as it is, once had a spectacular inception. But God has neither beginning nor end. He is utterly beyond any frame of reference that we have or can even logically theorize about.

We cannot begin to grasp the concept of an all-powerful Being who lives for endless ages. We can only say like Job, "How great is God—beyond our understanding! The number of his years is past finding out" (Job 36:26 NIV). In fact, for God to be God, He *has* to be beyond our understanding. If we could understand Him, we'd be omnipotent (all-knowing) like Him.

And of course we're not. He is, as Job said, a mystery past finding out.

Some people ask, "Who made God?" The logical answer is that no one made God. If some other being had made God, then *that* being would be God. And we'd still be left wondering where *that* being came from. But the Lord tells us, "I am the First and the Last. I am the one and only God" (Isaiah 44:6 nirv).

Discussion Questions

1. Do you think humans can grasp an infinite God? Why or why not?
2. Why must God *not* be finite or understandable?
3. What do you think God did before creating the universe?
4. Why couldn't some other being have created God?

3.

HOW CAN I BELIEVE IN SOMETHING I CAN'T SEE?

Christ is the exact likeness of God, who can't be seen.
COLOSSIANS 1:15 NIrv

You can believe in an invisible God because the evidence of His existence is all around you in the things He created. This not only gives us an idea of His majestic power, but a glimpse of His divine attributes as well. Still, He knew that human beings could easily misinterpret the evidence and end up, as many did, worshipping idols instead. That is why God sent His Son, Jesus Christ, to earth—to show us *exactly* what He is like.

God Himself can't be seen, but Christ is His "exact likeness." Jesus told His disciples, "'If you really knew me, you would know my Father also. From now on, you do know him. And you have seen him.' Philip said, 'Lord, show us the Father. That will be enough for us.' Jesus answered, 'Don't you know me, Philip? I have been among you such a long time! Anyone who has seen me has seen the Father'" (John 14:7–9 NIrv). The Bible further tells us that Christ "is the image of God" (2 Corinthians 4:4 NIV) and "radiates God's own glory and expresses the very character of God" (Hebrews 1:3 NLT).

God is love, and Jesus is like His Father in every way. By living a love-filled life here on earth, in plain view day after day, Christ showed what God is like in real time. Through His actions, Jesus demonstrated that God is a caring God—that He is concerned with people's struggles and trials and temptations. By constantly healing their sicknesses, He showed that God is concerned for our sufferings. By dying for our sins, Jesus proved how far God was willing to go to bring us back into His presence.

His entire life, Jesus Christ showed us what God is like.

DISCUSSION QUESTIONS

1. How has someone who has seen Jesus seen God?
2. Which of Jesus' actions show you God's most tender love?
3. Which of Jesus' words or actions show you God's love for justice?

4.

How Did God Create the Universe and Our World?

*By faith we understand that the universe was formed
at God's command, so that what is seen was not
made out of what was visible.*

HEBREWS 11:3 NIV

The Bible opens with these sweeping words: "In the beginning God created the heavens and the earth" (Genesis 1:1 NKJV). The rest of Genesis chapter 1 explains how life on Earth was formed, but to get back to the beginning: How exactly was the cosmos itself created? Did it resemble the scenario called the big bang? We don't know. God simply commanded and the universe with all its hundreds of billions of galaxies came into being. "The LORD merely spoke, and the heavens were created. He breathed the word, and all the stars were born" (Psalm 33:6 NLT).

As for how planet Earth was created, the Bible says that God spoke it into existence as well. "He spoke, and the world came into being. He commanded, and it stood firm" (Psalm 33:9 NIrV). The fact that Earth is spoken of as "formless" in the beginning (Genesis 1:2) may indicate that it was still coalescing into a globe at that early stage.

According to Genesis 1:14–19, the light from the sun, the moon, and the stars appeared in Earth's sky on the fourth day of Creation. Many Christians therefore believe that this was the day that the entire rest of the universe was created. This is not the *only* interpretation, however. Others believe that Genesis 1 is arranged according to alternating themes (days one and four—light; days two and five—seas; and days three and six—land) and wasn't intended to describe a precise chronological order.

Also, there are differing views about whether the days of Creation were six twenty-four-hour days or six great ages in the world's history. Both young and old earth creationists, while describing possible scenarios, seek to remain true to the scriptures, and there is much to commend both views. The important thing they agree on is that it was *God* who created everything.

Discussion Questions

1. Can you imagine how God could *speak* matter into existence?
2. How does this change your perception of God's power?
3. What order do you think God created things in?

5.

CAN THE BIBLE AND SCIENCE BE RECONCILED?

"I am the LORD, the Maker of all things,
who stretches out the heavens, who spreads out the earth
by myself. . .who overthrows the learning of the wise
and turns it into nonsense."
ISAIAH 44:24–25 NIV

Christians have several explanations for how the biblical accounts of Creation can be reconciled with science. The first position, young earth creationism, considers the seven *days* of Creation to be understood literally. They believe that the earth is less than ten thousand years old and reject all dating methods that indicate ages of billions of years. When the Bible and science disagree, they consider science to be pseudoscience—no matter how many learned men espouse it. They believe that this maxim applies: "They have rejected the word of the LORD. Are they so wise after all?" (Jeremiah 8:9 NLT).

In contrast, old earth creationists accept the great ages that the various scientific dating methods render. They believe that the testimony of the earth in an ancient geological record must affect our understanding of Genesis. They agree with Job who said, "Speak to the earth, and it will teach you" (Job 12:8 NKJV). Like the young earth creationists, they reject the theory of evolution but believe that God *continually* created new species at key points down through the ages. They point out that new species invariably appear in the fossil record suddenly and fully formed, not from pre-existing life forms.

Still other Christians are theistic evolutionists who believe that evolution explains how life began. They maintain, however, that God initiated the process and was intimately involved in guiding it every step of the way. Some believers in intelligent evolution reject the traditional Darwinian model of change by chance mutations, and explain that the way evolution *really* works is far more ingenious. They insist that an intelligent designer had to have created living organisms to make them capable of adapting the way they do.

No matter which model you believe best reconciles science and faith in God, remember: "Nothing that has been made was made without him" (John 1:3 NIrV).

DISCUSSION QUESTIONS

1. Which explanation, in your opinion, best reconciles the Bible and science?
2. How much have you studied each of the different options?
3. How important to your faith is understanding this issue?

6.

ARE THE BIBLE'S HISTORICAL RECORDS ACCURATE?

*For we have not followed cunningly devised fables,
when we made known unto you the power and coming of
our Lord Jesus Christ, but were eyewitnesses of his majesty.*
2 PETER 1:16 KJV

The Bible's historical accounts have been repeatedly confirmed by archaeology, down to the tiniest details, constantly confounding its critics and proving that the writers of the scriptures were accurate chroniclers of historical events. Those intrigued by this subject should begin by reading *Halley's Bible Handbook*. If you're interested in learning even more, you'll be fascinated by Kenneth Kitchen's volume, *On the Reliability of the Old Testament*.

Almost all Bible scholars acknowledge that the books of the Bible have been proven to be literal, chronological history as early as the mention of the city of Ur in Genesis 11:28—which has been discovered and excavated. Writing and record keeping began very early in human civilization, and those who wrote the historical books of the Bible were eyewitnesses to the events. Or they compiled their accounts from official records, which they cited as sources. We often read statements like "The rest of the events in Rehoboam's reign. . .are recorded in *The Book of the History of the Kings of Judah*" (1 Kings 14:29 NLT).

For their part, the Gospel writers were eyewitnesses

of Jesus' life, death, burial, and resurrection. The apostle John witnessed Jesus' death on the cross and wrote, "The man who saw it has given testimony. . . . He knows that he tells the truth" (John 19:35 NIV). Peter, who had seen and spoken with Jesus after His resurrection, stated, "God raised him from the dead. We are witnesses of this" (Acts 3:15 NIrV). Luke is widely recognized as a first-rate historian. He traveled to Israel to interview eyewitnesses and "carefully investigated everything from the beginning" (Luke 1:3 NLT). Time and again when one of Luke's statements in his Gospel or Acts was called into question, it was later validated by a new archaeological discovery.

DISCUSSION QUESTIONS

1. Do you know of cases where archaeology proved the Bible to be true?
2. What does all this archaeological evidence mean?
3. What weight do eyewitness testimonies have in a court case?
4. What are your thoughts on the first four verses in Luke's Gospel?

7.

Why Did God Create Us?

Thou art worthy, O Lord. . .for thou hast created all things, and for thy pleasure they are and were created.
REVELATION 4:11 KJV

The entire universe, this world and everything in it—including human beings, was created to give God pleasure. All these things please Him greatly and are the expressions of a loving Master Artist. But humans are His masterpiece, since we are the only beings of which it is said, "God created man in his own image" (Genesis 1:27 KJV).

We not only please God, but we are so important to Him that the very planet we live on was created for our benefit. When God formed the earth "He didn't create it to be empty. Instead, he formed it for people to live on" (Isaiah 45:18 NIRV). Solomon wrote in Proverbs, "The LORD by wisdom founded the earth" (3:19 NKJV), and a few chapters later he personified Wisdom who was with God at the beginning of time. Wisdom declares, "His whole world filled me with joy. I took delight in all human beings" (8:31 NIRV). Imagine! The Wisdom of God *delighted* in us and found *joy* that we inhabited the world.

The fact that humankind has chosen to turn away from the Lord is therefore a deep source of grief to Him. The beautiful plan that He had for us was marred by the disobedience of the first humans, Adam and Eve, and we've all inherited their inclination to sin. We choose our own selfish paths. God longed to gather us into His arms like the Father welcoming back the prodigal son, so He set in motion His plan: He sent His Son Jesus Christ into our world to make things right between us. Once again, the God who created you "will take great delight in you. . .he. . .will rejoice over you" (Zephaniah 3:17 NIV).

DISCUSSION QUESTIONS

1. How do you feel about God's reason for creating you?
2. How deeply do you believe that God *delights* in you?
3. How did Jesus complete God's original plan for humanity?

8.

Does God Ever Make Mistakes?

*Then the LORD saw that the wickedness of man was great.
. . . And the LORD was sorry that He had made man on
the earth, and He was grieved in His heart.*
Genesis 6:5–6 NKJV

When they read that "the LORD was sorry that He
had made man on the earth," many people think that
God realized that he'd made a mistake in creating us.
That's not so. The God who created *us* with emotions
is *Himself* an emotional being. He is all-wise and true,
but He is not "pure logic." He is capable of experiencing deep love, joy, happiness, anger, sorrow, and even
regret. In the above example, God was filled with sorrow over humankind's wickedness. He was grieved at
the very core of His being.

Sin still causes God deep emotional pain. Paul
warned us not to "grieve the Holy Spirit of God" who
lives in our hearts (Ephesians 4:30 NIV). Sin not only
causes God grief; but if we continue our willful actions,
as much as it hurts Him, He will chastise us and allow
us to suffer in order to persuade us to change.

God has always made it plain what His will is and
promises that if we obey Him, He'll bless us, but if
we sin, he'll *remove* His blessing. This happened several times in the Bible. For example, God would have
established Saul's house as a lasting dynasty had he
obeyed (1 Samuel 13:14). But when Saul continuously
disobeyed, "the LORD regretted that He had made Saul

king over Israel" (1 Samuel 15:35 NKJV) and removed him from the throne.

It works the other way also. Even though people have been willful and disobedient, God is moved to compassion if they have a change of heart. God had threatened to destroy wicked Nineveh, but when its people repented, He *didn't* destroy it. As Jonah told God, "I knew that you are a gracious and compassionate God, slow to anger and abounding in love, a God who relents from sending calamity" (Jonah 4:2 NIV).

DISCUSSION QUESTIONS

1. Do you picture God as emotional? Why or why not?
2. How can God experience regret if He doesn't make mistakes?
3. Do you believe God's blessings are contingent upon our obedience? Why?
4. Which four emotions in Jonah 4:2 caused God to relent?

9.

Does God Actually Get Angry? Why?

They defiled themselves by what they did;
by their deeds they prostituted themselves.
Therefore the Lord was angry with his people.
Psalm 106:39–40 NIV

Yes, God actually gets angry. He experiences the full range of emotions. Unfortunately, some people have been taught that God is angry *all* the time and has a very severe sense of justice. The resultant fear causes some people to develop a rigid religiosity or to become frustrated at their inability to please God. Some believers trade the concept of a perpetually angry God for one who is *always* compassionate and *never* angry. Both extremes are unscriptural. While it is true that "God is love" (1 John 4:16 KJV), the very fact that He *is* love means that He hates evil and injustice. Even Jesus became angry with hard-hearted hypocrites (Mark 3:5).

In the Old Testament, God's people repeatedly abandoned Him to worship idols of demons. They worshipped idols and degraded themselves both spiritually and physically in lascivious rites. This made the Lord angry (Judges 2:19–20; 2 Kings 17:17–18). It takes a *lot* to arouse God to wrath and judgment, however. Even after people engaged in idolatrous worship, the Lord sent prophets to warn them. "But they mocked God's messengers. . .until the wrath of the Lord was aroused against his people and there was no remedy" (2 Chronicles 36:16 NIV). Even God's long-suffering patience has its limits.

It also angers God when His people knowingly violate the laws he's given them and treat others cruelly and unfairly. God has warned many times that He is the avenger of the orphan, the widow, and the poor; so flagrant violators are without excuse. It grieves God to see the helpless being oppressed. It grieves Him to see us living wantonly, hurting ourselves and others, and willfully rejoicing in evil. These sins stir up God's wrath (Romans 2:4–6; Colossians 3:5–6).

Rather than question whether God has a *right* to get angry, people would do well to examine their hearts and cease from stubbornly doing things that grieve Him.

DISCUSSION QUESTIONS

1. Do you believe that God actually becomes angry?
2. Do you believe that God has a *right* to experience anger?
3. Do you think that God becomes angry *easily*, or that he's very patient?
4. What kinds of sins do you think anger God the most?

10.

How Was the Bible Written?

*For prophecy never came by the will of man, but holy men
of God spoke as they were moved by the Holy Spirit.*
2 PETER 1:21 NKJV

God uses words to communicate His thoughts to us,
and through the ages He chose people as His mouth-
pieces. "God...spoke...to the fathers by the prophets"
(Hebrews 1:1 NKJV), and as He spoke to their hearts,
the prophets said the words out loud. Abraham was
one such prophet (Genesis 20:7); and many centuries
before his day, humankind had learned how to create
written records. A careful examination of the book of
Genesis shows that it was written in stages, with each
generation of Abraham's family recording their story
for future generations. Contrary to some critics, the
Bible is not a collection of folktales passed down by
word of mouth for countless generations—and, so
they say, garbled over the centuries—before finally
being written.

Not all the prophets could read and write, however,
so a group of educated scribes were often given this
task. For example, when Baruch the scribe was asked
how Jeremiah's prophecies came to be, he explained,
"He pronounced all these words unto me with his
mouth, and I wrote them with ink in the book"
(Jeremiah 36:18 KJV).

A great creative explosion of God's Word happened in Moses' day. These writings, from Genesis to

Deuteronomy, were called the Law, and later writers added new scrolls to the collection. Not only were the words of the prophets recorded, but diligent scribes wrote accounts drawn from the official chronicles of Israel's kings. Inspired musicians like King David wrote psalms (songs) to praise God. All these scrolls were gathered and carefully guarded. Since these writings were the very Word of God, scribes copied each letter out by hand, reverently and painstakingly. All of these scrolls were called the Scriptures (the Writings), and as Paul tells us, "All Scripture is given by inspiration of God" (2 Timothy 3:16 NKJV).

DISCUSSION QUESTIONS

1. Writing existed before Abraham's day. What does this mean?
2. How can even historical records be the Word of God?
3. Why is the book of Psalms also considered scripture?
4. What part did scribes play in the formation of the Bible?

11.

How Do We Know That the Bible Is God's Word?

He gave his people good promises through his servant Moses. Every single word of those promises has come true.
1 KINGS 8:56 NIrV

What compels us to believe that the Bible is the inspired Word of God? There are several reasons, and the first one is obvious: fulfilled prophecies. Only an all-knowing God could predict the future hundreds of years before it happened. Once, God challenged the idolaters' "god" by saying that if he truly was divine, he should predict the future. "Yes, let them foretell what will come" (Isaiah 44:7 NIV). Of course, their false god couldn't. Only the Lord could, and in the following verses, God proceeded to call a Persian king *by name*—Cyrus—and describe how he'd conquer the Babylonian Empire and set the Jewish exiles free (Isaiah 44:28; 45:1–13). God stated this before Cyrus was even *born*, before the Babylonians ruled the world, and before the Jews were even exiles in Babylon!

The Bible contains hundreds more prophecies that were later fulfilled down to the details. These prophecies were often made hundreds of years before the event happened, before the person mentioned was even born. For example, Jesus' birth, ministry, death, burial, and resurrection fulfilled dozens of ancient prophecies. In Psalm 22 David describes the Messiah's crucifixion a thousand years before Christ's birth.

Isaiah 53 describes Jesus' trial and burial in chilling detail. The odds against these many, detailed prophecies being fulfilled in one man's life are astronomical. To learn more, read Josh McDowell's classic volume, *Evidence That Demands a Verdict*.

Another compelling proof that the Bible is God's Word is that it has the power to transform people's lives. Jesus' teachings on love, forgiveness, generosity, and faith have inspired millions and rescued ruined lives from the brink. They are exactly what we'd expect the message of a loving God to be. As people in Jesus' day exclaimed, "No man ever spoke like this Man!" (John 7:46 NKJV). See also Mark 1:22 and Luke 24:32.

DISCUSSION QUESTIONS

1. Why are the predictions of "psychics" often so vague and ambiguous?
2. Have you ever read Isaiah 53? Read it now and discuss it.
3. How has God's Word changed your life and others' lives?
4. Why do *you* believe that the Bible is God's Word?

12.

DID THE MIRACLES IN THE BIBLE REALLY HAPPEN?

*"Men of Israel, listen to this! . . . God did miracles,
wonders and signs among you through Jesus.
You yourselves know this."*
ACTS 2:22 NIrV

God simply spoke the word and hundreds of billions of galaxies came into being, so it shouldn't be hard for us to believe that He can continue to do *much smaller* miracles. Nevertheless, many people are skeptical because miracles are not everyday occurrences. Generally, the world runs the way God set it up, with gravity tugging on our toes, the seasons changing, and sunrise and sunset happening like clockwork. A miracle, by definition, defies the laws of nature. But God is capable of overriding His own *existing* laws to bring about new results.

Take the parting of the Red Sea: the Bible states, "The LORD caused the sea to go back by a strong east wind" (Exodus 14:21 NKJV), and when the Israelites crossed the sea bed, "the waters were a wall to them on their right hand and on their left" (14:22 NKJV). A few verses later, Moses, an eyewitness to the event, explained, "The depths congealed in the heart of the sea" (15:8 NKJV). Congealed means "hardened." That doesn't mean the water had frozen like ice, but it *does* mean something out of the ordinary was happening to the water to cause it to stand stiff like walls. God's normal laws of physics were responding to His awesome power.

It would be nice if we could always understand *how* miracles happened; but whether we can or not, in both the Old and New Testaments, multitudes of witnesses *saw* them happen. Jesus repeatedly performed miracles in front of crowds of thousands (John 6:2). When He healed a blind, mute man "all the multitudes were amazed" (Matthew 12:23 NKJV). What's more, when Peter told the crowds that Jesus had done miracles, he confidently stated, "You yourselves know this" (Acts 2:22 NIrV). Indeed they *did*. After Peter and John healed a lame man, even their exasperated enemies confessed, "We can't deny that they have performed a miraculous sign, and everybody in Jerusalem knows about it" (Acts 4:16 NLT).

DISCUSSION QUESTIONS

1. Why isn't it always possible to understand *how* miracles happen?
2. What is the purpose of God doing miracles?
3. What effect did miracles have on the crowds who saw them?
4. Have you ever witnessed a miracle?

13.

WEREN'T MOST "MIRACLES" JUST NATURAL EVENTS?

Right away the water that was coming down the river stopped flowing. It piled up far away at a town called Adam near Zarethan.
JOSHUA 3:16 NIrv

Some people, although they believe that the Bible describes historical events, have difficulty accepting the supernatural aspects. They attempt to come up with rational explanations for how the miracles "actually" happened. And some of their theories are more unbelievable than the Bible's statement that God did a miracle. Often they have to downgrade the event and change some of its details to make it "fit" their explanation.

Nevertheless, God sometimes does use natural means to accomplish His will—and *still* does to this day. A good example is when the Israelites prepared to cross the Jordan River into Canaan. Normally the Jordan isn't very wide, but it was springtime and the river was swollen with rain and melted snow. It overflowed its banks and filled the flood plains. But the instant the priests stepped into the river, the water level dropped until the riverbed was empty. Only after *all* the Israelites had crossed did the river start flowing again (Joshua 3–4).

How did God do this? Well, the Bible tells us that "the water. . .piled up far away at a town called Adam" (Joshua 3:16 NIrv). Adam was twenty miles upstream from Jericho. The river gorge is narrow there, and sometimes the cliffs collapse and a landslide dams the river. This happened in 1927, blocking the Jordan for twenty hours. How would God have caused a landslide in Joshua's day? It could've been the heavy spring rains. Or very likely, God sent an earthquake to shake the hills, as Psalm 114:3–7 seems to imply.

Even if God used natural means, you have to admit that the *exact timing* of the river drying up was a huge miracle. And speaking of timing, the instant the last Israelite priest walked out of the riverbed, the Jordan flooded back again.

DISCUSSION QUESTIONS

1. Does God sometimes use natural means to perform His will?
2. How was the drying of the Jordan River still a miracle?
3. Can *all* the miracles in the Bible be explained?
4. What "miracle of timing" has God done in *your* life?

14.

ARE THERE MISTAKES IN THE BIBLE?

The law of the LORD is perfect, converting the soul;
the testimony of the LORD is sure, making wise the simple.
PSALM 19:7 NKJV

Every word in scripture, from Genesis to Revelation, was inspired by God. "All Scripture is God-breathed" (2 Timothy 3:16 NIV) and is therefore perfect, because God is perfect. He doesn't get His facts wrong, He doesn't make mistakes, and He doesn't lie (Numbers 23:19). Scripture, therefore, doesn't contain mistakes. Conservative Bible scholars agree that God's Word, in its original autographs, was completely error-free.

The expression, "in its original autographs," refers to the *original* copies of God's Word when it was written down. No Bible scholar disputes the fact that scribes occasionally introduced small errors into the manuscripts later as they were hand copying them. In some cases, a letter was accidentally dropped from the text. But for the most part, these are mere variations in spelling and grammar and don't change the meaning of the text at all.

Because of this, Bible critics have said that we have no way of knowing whether the scriptures we have today are true to their original versions. Much of this criticism stopped when the Dead Sea Scrolls were discovered in Israel in 1946–48. Clay jars full of amazingly preserved scrolls were discovered— among them a complete scroll of the prophet Isaiah.

This scroll dates to one hundred years before Christ and is virtually *identical* to the book of Isaiah that we have today—over two thousand years later. This level of preservation is a testament to the great care scribes took while copying God's Word.

In contrast, some critics believe that a few of the common expressions used in the Bible represent errors. For example, the Bible often talks about "sunrise," even though we know that the sun *doesn't* rise. Its apparent rising and setting is due to Earth turning on its axis. Yet we still use the same expression today. Everyone understands what we mean, and not even the most nit-picky person feels compelled to insist that *we* shouldn't say "sunrise."

DISCUSSION QUESTIONS

1. Do you believe there are mistakes in the scriptures? What kind?
2. Do you believe the Bible was perfect in its original autographs?
3. What factors would cause a scribe to make copying errors?
4. Should God use common, unscientific expressions? Why or why not?

15.

DON'T THE GOSPELS CONTRADICT EACH OTHER?

Many people have set out to write accounts about the events that have been fulfilled among us. They used the eyewitness reports circulating among us.
LUKE 1:1–2 NLT

Matthew and John were both eyewitnesses of Jesus' ministry, death, and resurrection; Mark was a disciple of Peter and wrote down his memoirs; Luke interviewed eyewitnesses. Each Gospel describes the events of Jesus' life from a slightly different perspective, and often one writer mentions incidents that the others didn't include. What raises questions, however, is when they describe the *same* event but seem to give conflicting accounts.

For example, Mark states that Jesus was crucified in "the third hour" (15:25 NKJV). In Jewish time, this is 9:00 a.m. He adds that "when the sixth hour had come, there was darkness over the whole land until the ninth hour" (15:33 NKJV). This was from noon until 3:00 p.m. However, John tells us that Jesus didn't even appear before Pilate until "about the sixth hour" (John 19:14 KJV). How could Jesus appear before Pilate for the first time at noon, when He was crucified three hours *earlier* at 9:00 a.m.?

The answer is simple: when John wrote his Gospel in the Roman city of Ephesus, he couldn't use Jewish time. His readers understood Roman timekeeping methods—and according to *them* "the sixth hour" was 6:00 a.m. That means it took about three hours for Jesus to stand trial before Pilate and carry His cross to Golgotha. This fits the timeline perfectly.

Another seeming contradiction is the women's early morning visit to Jesus' tomb. Mark 16:5 tells us they saw one "young man" sitting in the tomb. But Luke 24:4 tells us they saw two angels standing. And John 20:12 tells us they saw two angels seated. Why the differences? Many Bible scholars have concluded that *two* groups of women visited the tomb at different times. We know also that Mary Magdalene saw the two angels on her *second* visit to the tomb. It takes study, but the differing accounts can be reconciled.

DISCUSSION QUESTIONS

1. What do you think about contradictions in the Gospels?
2. Can *all* such differences be explained? Why or why not?
3. How important are such issues to your faith?

16.

WHO EXACTLY IS JESUS?

*"Let everyone in Israel know for certain that God has
made this Jesus, whom you crucified,
to be both Lord and Messiah!"*
ACTS 2:36 NLT

Jesus was born to a young Jewish woman named Mary,
having been conceived in His mother's womb by the
Holy Spirit. Although Jesus appeared to be a normal
man, He was also the eternal Son of God who had
existed with His Father before the world began (Luke
1:26–38; John 1:1–14). Jesus would have been stoned
had He declared this openly (John 10:29–33), so He
usually called Himself "the Son of Man"—a lesser-
known reference to His eternal relationship with His
Father (Daniel 7:13–14).

God had made many promises in the Old
Testament that He would send the Messiah (the
"Anointed One") to deliver His people. The title
"Christ" is the Greek translation of Messiah. Most
Jews in Jesus' day expected the Messiah to be a great
warrior king who would deliver them militarily from
their oppressors and set up His kingdom.

David had been Israel's king a thousand years earlier, and God had promised that his kingdom would
endure forever (2 Samuel 7:16). But now Israel had *no*
king and was ruled by foreigners. The Jews of Jesus' day
longed for a great king of the royal house—the "Son
of David"—to rise. Mary and Joseph were descendants

of David, and the Jews often called Jesus the Son of David (Luke 2:1–7; 18:38).

Also, Moses, the greatest prophet Israel had ever known, had promised that God would raise up a new Prophet like him to teach them to follow God (Deuteronomy 18:18–19; Acts 3:22–26). Some Jews thought the king and the prophet would be two different people, but others believed correctly that they would be one and the same (John 6:14–15).

Jesus is *all* these things: He is the Son of God, the Son of Man, the Son of David, and the promised Prophet.

DISCUSSION QUESTIONS

1. How is Jesus both a normal man and the Son of God?
2. How did Jesus fulfill the "Son of David" prophecy?
3. How did Jesus fulfill Moses' prophecy about the Prophet?
4. Why did the Jews *not* expect the Messiah to fulfill Isaiah 53?

17.

Why Did Jesus Go Around Healing People?

Jesus. . .went about doing good and healing all who were oppressed by the devil, for God was with Him.
Acts 10:38 NKJV

As Jesus traveled around the towns and villages of Judea and Galilee teaching people about the kingdom of God, He was constantly healing their sicknesses—fevers, leprosy, and other diseases. He gave sight to the blind, hearing to the deaf, and even raised the dead back to life. Many Jews had no idea that the Messiah, when He came, would do such things—but the scriptures had clearly foretold that He would (Isaiah 29:18; 35:5–6; 42:7).

When John the Baptist began questioning whether Jesus was the promised Messiah, Jesus sent this message back with John's disciples: "Go and tell John the things which you hear and see: the blind see and the lame walk; the lepers are cleansed and the deaf hear; the dead are raised up" (Matthew 11:4–5 NKJV). Jesus fully expected that John would understand that these miracles were proof that He *was* the Messiah.

These things were part of Jesus' ministry for two reasons: First, they proved that *God* had given power to Jesus. When Jesus healed a blind man, His religious enemies cross-examined the man, insisting that Jesus was a sinful, godless person. The formerly blind man wisely replied, "Since the world began was it not heard that any man opened the eyes of one that was born blind. If this man were not of God, he could do nothing" (John 9:32–33 KJV). Jesus' astonishing miracles were proof that He was the Messiah. From the beginning of Jesus' ministry, "many believed in his name, when they saw the miracles which he did" (John 2:23 KJV).

The second reason that Jesus did healing miracles was that He *cared* for people. In a day when so many were sick and doctors so few and their skills so limited, healing people clearly demonstrated God's love for them.

DISCUSSION QUESTIONS

1. How were healing miracles a sign that Jesus was the Messiah?
2. How did miracles prove that God had sent Jesus?
3. Do you believe that God still does healing miracles today?

18.

HOW COULD JESUS BE HUMAN
YET NEVER SIN?

*We have a high priest who has been tempted in every way,
just as we are. But he did not sin.*
HEBREWS 4:15 NIrV

Ever since Adam and Eve, people have been born with
a sinful nature—meaning that they're inclined to be
selfish and to do their own thing. People don't *have*
to sin, however, and often they *do* choose to do good
and noble and kind things. The problem is that people
don't *always* choose what's right. When tempted, they
often give in. Jesus was fully human, yet He chose to do
the loving, unselfish thing *every* time. He was tempted
just like every human is, but He consistently chose to
obey God (John 8:29). Jesus could do this because He
was *fully* committed to doing God's will. As He said,
"I do not seek My own will but the will of the Father"
(John 5:30 NKJV).

Jesus wasn't just tempted to sin once or twice.
Some people think that the only times He was
tested was when the devil tempted Him in the desert
(Matthew 4:1–10) and when He wanted to avoid crucifixion (Matthew 26:39). As we know, being human
means that we're tempted constantly. We face choices
between selfish or unselfish actions every single day.
And Jesus was tempted in every way that we are.

Even though He never gave in to sin, it was
important that He was repeatedly tested and required

to constantly resist temptation. "He himself suffered when he was tempted. Now he is able to help others who are being tempted" (Hebrews 2:18 NIrv). Like us, Jesus knows how difficult it can be to resist temptation. He knows that it can sometimes seem overwhelming. He has compassion when we fall—or nearly fall. But He serves as an example to us: we don't *have* to sin (1 Corinthians 10:13; Titus 2:11–12).

DISCUSSION QUESTIONS

1. Is being *tempted* to sin, a sin? Why or why not?
2. Do you believe Jesus was tempted in *every* way like we are?
3. Was it impossible for Jesus to sin, or did He choose not to?
4. How do Jesus' sufferings help Him have compassion on us?

19.

How Could Jesus Be Both God *and* Man?

Though he was God, he did not think of equality with God as something to cling to. Instead, he gave up his divine privileges. . .and was born as a human being.
Philippians 2:6–7 nlt

Jesus had a mother, Mary, and He was fully human. He became hungry and ate, He became thirsty and drank, and He became weary and slept. If it wasn't for the incredible miracles that He performed and His amazing teachings, He could have passed for just another Jewish man in the crowd. But Jesus was *more* than an ordinary man. He was also God's own Son. When asked bluntly if He was the Son of God, Jesus replied, "Yes. It is just as you say" (Matthew 26:64 nirv).

But then Jesus took it a step further when He stated, "I and my Father are one" (John 10:30 kjv). The apostle John, at the beginning of his Gospel, tells us that "the Word was with God, and the Word was God" (John 1:1 niv). Jesus *is* God. That's why when Jesus showed Thomas that He was alive again after being crucified, Thomas said to Him, "My Lord and my God" (John 20:28 kjv). Also, Isaiah said that the Savior would be born as a man but would be called, "The mighty God, The everlasting Father, The Prince of Peace" (Isaiah 9:6 kjv).

Paul explains that "in Christ lives all the fullness of God in a human body" (Colossians 2:9 nlt). This leads to the question: How can the God who created the entire universe be contained in a mortal body? After all, when Solomon built the temple, he confessed that even the heaven of heavens couldn't contain God—how much less a temple (1 Kings 8:27). The answer lies in the meaning of "fullness." It doesn't mean that every iota of the immensity of God the Father dwelt in Christ's body. Rather, it means that the Spirit of Jesus in His body was just as fully God as the Father was. When God took on bodily form, He was still God.

DISCUSSION QUESTIONS

1. Do you believe that Jesus was fully and completely human?
2. What do you understand Jesus' title "the Son of God" to mean?
3. How could all "the fullness of God" dwell in a human body?
4. Read Genesis 1:1 and Colossians 1:15–16. What do you think?

20.

WHAT IS THE TRINITY?

*"Go therefore and make disciples of all the nations,
baptizing them in the name of the Father
and of the Son and of the Holy Spirit."*
MATTHEW 28:19 NKJV

Before Christ, the Israelites correctly understood that
there was one God. Moses wrote, "Hear, O Israel: The
LORD our God, the LORD is one" (Deuteronomy 6:4
NIV). However, from the very beginning, the scriptures talked about the Spirit of God as a distinct entity
(Genesis 1:2). The Israelites talked about the "Spirit
of the LORD" taking action (2 Kings 2:16), and how
God sent His Spirit (Psalm 104:30). Jesus also talked
about God sending the Holy Spirit (John 14:26). Yet
this distinction did not cause the Jews to doubt that
there was one God. God's Spirit was *part* of Him and
one with Him.

When Jesus declared that He was the Son of God,
His Jewish enemies picked up stones to throw at Him.
They accused Him of blasphemy, saying, "You, a mere
man, claim to be God" (John 10:33 NLT). This *is*, in
fact, what the New Testament claims. Paul wrote that
"God was manifested in the flesh" (1 Timothy 3:16
NKJV). The book of Revelation makes it clear that
Jesus and the eternal God are one and the same. God
declared, "I am the Alpha and the Omega." And Jesus
also declared, "I am the Alpha and the Omega. . .the
Beginning and the End" (1:8; 22:13 NIV).

Furthermore, Jesus said that He, Jesus, would send the Holy Spirit "from the Father" (John 15:26). Here are three distinct entities, all of whom are God. The evidence is overwhelming for Christians: God the Father is God, and the Spirit of God is also God, and the Son is also God—yet there is only *one* God—so these three beings have to be differing aspects of a triune God. This is where the doctrine of the Trinity comes from.

DISCUSSION QUESTIONS

1. Do you believe that God and His Spirit are one?
2. Do you believe that Jesus is God? Why or why not?
3. Do you feel the expression "triune God" adequately sums things up?
4. What are some simple comparisons that could help explain the Trinity?

21.

WHO OR WHAT IS THE HOLY SPIRIT?

Who can know the thoughts of another person?
Only a person's own spirit can know them. In the same
way, only the Spirit of God knows God's thoughts.
1 CORINTHIANS 2:11 NIrv

The Holy Spirit is the Lord's own Spirit. His Spirit is not an "it." He is not some impersonal power or force. The Spirit is God Himself, the third Person of the Trinity. The Spirit of the Lord is omniscient and knows everything the Father knows. He is omnipotent, was actively engaged in the creation of the universe, and still does miracles today. He is omnipresent and fills all space and time. There is no place where we can go to escape from the presence of God's Spirit (Psalm 139:7–12).

When God wished to give power to chosen rulers, He filled them with His Holy Spirit. David is an example of this: "From that day on the Spirit of the LORD came powerfully upon David" (1 Samuel 16:13 NIV). It happened to Samson as well (Judges 14:6). God also sent His Spirit into the prophets to inspire them to speak His words. Before He ascended to heaven, Jesus promised His disciples that He would send the Holy Spirit—not only to be *with* them, but to live *in* their very hearts (John 14:17). In the past, God had only sent His Spirit upon key people. With the birth of the Church, however, He promised to send His Spirit upon all believers.

Jesus explained that "the Spirit of truth" testifies that He is the Savior (John 15:26). In fact, the Holy Spirit is the one who causes us to experience a spiritual birth: "the Spirit alone gives eternal life" (John 6:63 NLT). When we become Christians, God sends His Spirit into our hearts to show that we belong to Him (Ephesians 1:13–14). The Holy Spirit also teaches us, comforts us, and gives us power to live the Christian life and to be a witness for Jesus (John 14:25–26; Acts 1:8).

DISCUSSION QUESTIONS

1. Do you envision the Spirit as a person or as a force?
2. Why do you think God's Spirit does so *much*?
3. What good things does the Holy Spirit do for you?
4. Why does God send His Spirit into your heart?
5. Has the Holy Spirit given *you* power? Explain.

22.

IS JESUS THE ONLY WAY TO GOD?

*Jesus told him, "I am the way, the truth, and the life.
No one can come to the Father except through me."*
JOHN 14:6 NLT

Yes, Jesus is the only way to God, His Father. Jesus said that He is *"the* way." He is not *a* way, one path among many that leads to eternal life. He is *the* way and *the* life. No one can come to God except through Jesus. Why? Because He is the only perfect, complete way of truth. Most religions teach *some* good morals and *some* truth about God—so you should respect them for that—but they have only part of the truth, and most also teach a great deal that is false. Therefore they can only take people *part*way to God. They can't take anyone all the way, because they can't get across the vast gulf of sin that separates God from humans.

Jesus is *the* truth because everything He taught is true with no error mixed in. Jesus is *the* way because when He died so that you could be forgiven, He created a way where there was no way—a bridge across the gap of sin—all the way to God. That's why Jesus is the only one who can give us eternal life with God in heaven.

This truth is consistently stated in the Bible. The first Christians proclaimed, "Salvation is found in no one else, for there is no other name under heaven given to mankind by which we must be saved" (Acts 4:12 NIV). No one else, no religious teacher or self-proclaimed savior, can save you. There is no other. The apostle Paul repeated, "There is one God, and one mediator between God and mankind, the man Christ Jesus" (1 Timothy 2:5 NIV). A mediator is someone who settles a dispute between two parties. In this case, the issue was sin, and Jesus was the *only* mediator who could make peace between us and God.

DISCUSSION QUESTIONS

1. Do most religions contain *some* kernel of truth? Why?
2. Which "paths" actually lead people the furthest astray?
3. What is the main reason that Jesus is *the* way to God?
4. What does it mean that Jesus is *the* truth?

23.

Aren't All Religions Basically the Same?

You believe that there is one God. You do well.
Even the demons believe—and tremble!
James 2:19 NKJV

All religions are *not* basically the same. For one thing, although some religions have relatively benign creeds, others contain very dark teachings and practices. In the Old Testament, the worship of Canaanite gods and goddesses often involved lascivious acts and human sacrifice. It was outright demonic (Deuteronomy 32:17; Psalm 106:37). Even though the worship of most Greek and Roman gods was not quite as evil, Paul said that "the sacrifices of pagans are offered to demons, not to God" (1 Corinthians 10:20 NIV).

These days, many religions teach that there is only one God and He alone is to be worshipped. This much is true, and they do well to believe that. However, almost all of them teach that people must do good deeds or works to "earn" salvation. God has nothing to do with saving them other than to act as a fair Judge and acknowledge that they lived a (mostly) righteous life. Many believe that God will weigh their bad and good deeds, and if the good outweighs the evil, they'll be allowed into heaven. They're not quite sure *what* constitutes a "passing mark," but hope the bar is 51 percent. . .or *less*.

The next logical leap in their "save-yourself religion" is that, in the end, it probably doesn't matter *what* someone believes—in one God or many gods or no god at all. As long as people live a more or less moral life, they're safe.

The Bible teaches that we're *not* saved by our good works, and that even the best of us have sinned and need to be forgiven. Salvation is not a do-it-yourself kit, but God mercifully forgiving your sins. If you put your faith in Jesus Christ and trust Him to save you, you'll be saved. Salvation is a gift. All you have to do is receive it.

DISCUSSION QUESTIONS

1. Which religions would you say are dark or immoral?
2. Which religions would you say have some good teachings?
3. How do even their "good" teachings lead people astray?
4. Can you do enough good deeds to earn eternal life?
5. How is Christianity different from all other religions?

24.

AREN'T ALL PEOPLE BASICALLY GOOD?

*There is not a just man on earth
who does good and does not sin.*
ECCLESIASTES 7:20 NKJV

Humankind was created in the image of God (Genesis 1:27), and though we've fallen from that original sinless state, we still retain the capacity to care, to nurture, and to protect. Even pagans and unbelievers are capable of loving acts. As Jesus pointed out, even a greedy, gouging tax collector loves those who love him. Pagans greet their friends. And otherwise evil fathers still provide food for their children (Matthew 5:46–47; 7:9–11). But humankind's nature has been greatly corrupted; and even the *good* we do is tainted by pride, selfishness, lust, jealousy, greed, and other selfish motivations. "If we say that we have no sin, we deceive ourselves" (1 John 1:8 KJV).

Some theologians used to think that humankind was already living in the millennium, heaven on earth. Then World War I happened. And the world has gotten much worse since then, with the horrors of the Holocaust, ethnic cleansing, and the inhuman cruelty of totalitarian regimes. If you spend time watching the news, talking to police officers, or walking the streets of your city—even in civilized countries—you'll realize just how sinful and selfish people can be. But sometimes it takes being the victim of a break-in or the target of malicious gossip to bring this point home.

However, don't decide that all people are totally evil, or that they think and do nothing but evil all the time. All human beings are capable of goodness. . . at times, and criminals, despots, and drug lords are not the *only* sinners. Sin means any kind of selfish behavior and law breaking—even the kind that happens in corporate offices and in the homes of upstanding citizens. After all, selfishness, grudges, and simmering anger are also sins.

DISCUSSION QUESTIONS

1. Are people basically good or selfish—or both?
2. How can selfish motivations color even the good we do?
3. Have you had a close look at the seamy side of your city?
4. Do even moral people in good homes sin? Why?

25.

WHAT IS SIN, AND WHY IS IT A BIG DEAL?

When desire has conceived, it gives birth to sin;
and sin, when it is full-grown, brings forth death.
JAMES 1:15 NKJV

The Bible tells us that "all have sinned, and come short of the glory of God" (Romans 3:23 KJV). We readily admit that God, to *be* God, must be perfect—and we're also aware that we're *not*. And we can certainly agree that we fall short of God's glory. On the other hand, many of us rationalize that, after all, we're "only human." We're fallible, weak mortals. We make mistakes. Yes, we have selfish motivations at times. But we don't like to consider these things "sins," at least not *serious* sins. To do so puts an unwanted dent in our self-esteem.

Some clarification will help bring this into focus: the Greek word for sin, *hamartanō*, means "to err, to miss the mark." So when the Bible says that we have all sinned, it's saying that none of us are perfectly good. Although we may *also* do good things *some*times and even attempt to live according to a good moral code, we know that our selfish nature *also* constantly asserts itself. We're all guilty of wrong thoughts and actions. We all miss the mark. With that in mind, we can probably agree that we're sinners. Now what?

We must come face-to-face with the destructive *end result* of sin. Sin may seem like a small, inconsequential thing now, but "sin, when it is full-grown, brings forth death" (James 1:15 NKJV). Or as the apostle Paul explained, the ultimate paycheck or wages of sin is death (Romans 6:23). In this life people may seem to be getting away with decades of sinful habits, but that's because the time of reckoning hasn't yet arrived. It's not yet payday. When *that* day finally arrives, people will find that the wage they have earned is death—eternal separation from God. *That* is why sin is so serious.

DISCUSSION QUESTIONS

1. Is being selfish and unloving "sin"—or is it just "being human"?
2. What is the definition of sin? Does that make us all sinners?
3. Why is the end result of sin so serious?

26.

WHY DID JESUS HAVE TO DIE ON THE CROSS?

"The life of the flesh is in the blood, and I have given it to you. . .to make atonement for your souls; for it is the blood that makes atonement for the soul."

LEVITICUS 17:11 NKJV

When Adam and Eve disobeyed God and ate the fruit of the tree of the knowledge of good and evil, they gained wisdom, true, but at a terrible price: they lost their innocence and now knew the difference between good and evil (Genesis 3:6, 22). Afterward when they disobeyed God, they were *aware* that they were doing wrong—yet they still chose it. They were accountable and judged guilty. Just as God had warned, they died spiritually, and we inherited their proclivity to sin. The Bible states, "The soul who sins shall die" (Ezekiel 18:20 NKJV).

God, however, longed for His people to repent so He could forgive them. He allowed them to substitute a sacrificial animal so they didn't have to die. This act of obedience demonstrated their acknowledgment of guilt, their repentance, their request for forgiveness, and their dependence upon the mercy of God. As the blood drained out of the sacrifice, it died and the price was paid. The blood had made "atonement"—which means "to cover" their sins—and God then forgave them. "The life of the flesh is in the blood" (Leviticus 17:11 NKJV), and "without the shedding of blood there is no forgiveness" (Hebrews 9:22 NIV).

However, the blood of sacrificial animals could never permanently atone for sin. People kept having to return with a new sacrifice to cover new disobediences. So God made one final sacrifice to forgive *all* our sins once and for all. He sent His only Son, Jesus, to die in our place. Jesus' lifeblood drained out of His body as the ultimate sacrificial offering, and "the blood of Jesus, his Son, purifies us from all sin" (1 John 1:7 NIV). See also 1 Peter 1:18–19.

DISCUSSION QUESTIONS

1. Why did God institute the practice of sacrificial offerings?
2. How does blood deal with the problem of sin?
3. Why were animal sacrifices only temporarily effective?
4. Why is Jesus called "the ultimate sacrifice"?

27.

DID JESUS ACTUALLY RISE FROM THE DEAD?

*He also presented Himself alive after
His suffering by many infallible proofs,
being seen by them during forty days.*
ACTS 1:3 NKJV

Our immortal spirit lives inside our mortal body, and after our body dies, our spirit lives on. But God doesn't intend our spirit to be detached from our bodies forever, floating around in some nebulous, intangible state. God intends for us to live here on earth in physical form. He has promised that He will bring our bodies back to life and reunite them with our spirits. He will also transform them from weak, *mortal* bodies into powerful, glorious, *immortal* bodies (1 Corinthians 15:12–57).

This is why it was important that Jesus' physical body be raised from the dead after He was crucified. And He *was.* After being resurrected on the third day, "He was seen by Peter and then by the Twelve. After that, he was seen by more than five hundred of his followers at one time" (1 Corinthians 15:5–6 NLT). It wasn't just the handful of women at His tomb on Sunday morning who witnessed that Jesus was alive again. He continued to show Himself day after day for forty days, to over five hundred of His disciples.

He also offered them many "infallible proofs." He needed to. After all, when the disciples first saw Jesus, they thought they were seeing a ghost—Jesus' *spirit.*

That's why He said, "It is I myself! Touch me and see; a ghost does not have flesh and bones, as you see I have" (Luke 24:39 NIV). And they *did* touch Him. Thomas, who wasn't present at that first meeting, insisted on poking his finger into Jesus' nail wounds to verify that it was actually Him (John 20:24–28). To further prove that He was not merely a spirit, but that He had a physical body, Jesus ate food while His disciples watched (Luke 24:41–43).

Jesus' resurrection demonstrated that He had power over death, and was *proof* that He was the Son of God (Romans 1:3–4; 6:9).

DISCUSSION QUESTIONS

1. Why will God give us immortal physical bodies?
2. Why was it important that Jesus' body be raised from the dead?
3. What proof did Jesus offer that He was alive again?
4. How did Jesus' resurrection prove that He was the Son of God?

28.

Do Heaven and Hell Really Exist?

*"Those who have done good will rise to experience
eternal life, and those who have continued in evil
will rise to experience judgment."*
John 5:29 NLT

Our spirits are eternal, and after our bodies have been
resurrected and reunited with our spirits, our entire
physical and spiritual being will live forever. Even
though our new bodies will be immortal and have
astonishing powers that we never dreamed of, they'll
still need a tangible place to exist for eternity. So yes,
both heaven and hell are *real* places. They are not mere
parables or metaphors for something else.

Heaven, the place where God dwells, is not pres-
ently on this earth. But one day the heavenly city,
New Jerusalem, *will* come down out of the heavens
and settle on this planet, and will remain here forever. God will actually dwell with humankind in this
physical world (Revelation 21:2–3, 10). This dwelling,
described as a "city," is also called God's "house," and
Jesus stated that it's real. He said, "In my Father's house
are many mansions: if it were not so, I would have told
you." He then added, "I go to prepare a place for you"
(John 14:2 KJV).

Likewise, hell, the eternal dwelling of the unre-
pentant, is a real, literal place. The Bible speaks of it
often, and although we don't know exactly *where* it is,
it's described as being someplace *outside* New Jerusalem

(Revelation 22:14–15). Some people believe that hell is inside the earth, but that is only a guess.

We can also be certain that there will be a Final Judgment when all the people who have ever lived appear before God to be judged (Matthew 25:31–46). Paul stated, "He has appointed a day on which He will judge the world. . . . He has given assurance of this" (Acts 17:31 NKJV). First comes the resurrection of the saved, and the resurrection of the unsaved is a thousand years later (Revelation 20:6, 11–15).

DISCUSSION QUESTIONS

1. Why will we require a tangible, real place to live in eternity?
2. Do you believe heaven and hell exist? Why or why not?
3. Do you think they are made of *ordinary* matter?
4. How is the Final Judgment part of this?

29.

WHAT IS HEAVEN LIKE?

*No eye has seen, no ear has heard, and no mind has
imagined what God has prepared for those who love him.*
1 CORINTHIANS 2:9 NLT

The final two chapters of Revelation describe heaven
in some detail. John tells us that it is a magnificent city
called New Jerusalem. "It shone with the glory of God,
and its brilliance was like that of a very precious jewel"
(Revelation 21:11 NIV). John also tells us that the city
was "of pure gold, as pure as glass" (v. 18 NIV) and had
a great, high wall around it. In verse 21 he describes
gates of giant pearls and a great street of pure gold. God
Himself dwells in the city with the redeemed saints of
all ages. And the city is *immense*! It's over a thousand
miles high, wide, and broad (Revelation 21–22).

Many Christians take these descriptions literally
and dream of living in mansions (John 14:2) along
streets of gold. Other believers, however, insist that
these descriptions are figurative. They point out that
many of the visions in the book of Revelation are highly
symbolic, and that this description of New Jerusalem
should be understood in the same way. For example, the
white robes that we wear symbolize our righteousness
(Revelation 19:8). Proponents of a figurative interpretation point out that 1 Corinthians 2:9 declares that no
one can imagine how wonderful heaven will be. More
literal Christians reply that, yes, this *was* the case when
Paul wrote it in AD 55, but John described heaven some

forty years later, in AD 95.

Despite these varying opinions, all Christians agree that heaven will be a truly wonderful place where we'll be reunited with departed loved ones and live in the presence of the Lord forever. "God shall wipe away all tears from their eyes; and there shall be no more death, neither sorrow, nor crying, neither shall there be any more pain" (Revelation 21:4 KJV).

DISCUSSION QUESTIONS

1. Do you believe the description of heaven is literal or symbolic? Why?
2. Why would God describe to us what heaven is like?
3. What are you looking forward to the most in heaven?

30.

WOULD A LOVING GOD SEND PEOPLE TO HELL?

*But he will pour out his anger and wrath
on those who. . .refuse to obey the truth and
instead live lives of wickedness.*

ROMANS 2:8 NLT

When Jesus described hell, He used the word *Gehenna* and said it was a place where "their worm does not die, and the fire is not quenched" (Mark 9:44 NKJV). *Gehenna* comes from *ge-hinnom* (the Valley of Hinnom), a truly evil place where in centuries past, idolaters cast their children into the flames while worshipping demonic idols (2 Chronicles 28:3). Later, godly Jews destroyed the idols (2 Kings 23:10) and turned the valley into Jerusalem's garbage dump—a place filled with burning trash and rotting, worm-riddled refuse. The apostle John further described Gehenna as a "lake of fire" (Revelation 20:15 KJV) into which the wicked will be cast and said that "the smoke of their torment will rise forever and ever" (Revelation 14:11 NLT).

Many Christians have difficulty believing that a God of love would actually make people suffer forever in a literal lake of burning sulfur. Billy Graham said that he thought that the fire was a burning thirst for God that can never be quenched. He added, "I think that hell. . .is separation from God forever." In other words, people end up not being with God in heaven because they willfully reject the truth then later regret their decision for all eternity.

Jesus said that it would be "more bearable" in the Day of Judgment (Matthew 10:15 NIV) for those who had not sinned as greatly as others. This is the whole purpose of the Last Judgment, to judge people for their deeds. God is just. He will certainly not cause everyone to suffer to the same extent as evil men like Hitler.

Whether you believe that hell is a lake of fire, a smoking garbage dump, or a lonely separation from God, know this: people *don't have to go there*! God offers us eternal salvation through Jesus Christ.

DISCUSSION QUESTIONS

1. Do you think the Bible's description of hell is literal or symbolic?
2. Why did God describe hell in such stark terms?
3. Will people's punishment there be measured and fair?
4. Why is hell called "the second death" (Revelation 21:8)?

31.

WHAT ABOUT PEOPLE WHO HAVE NEVER HEARD OF JESUS?

If our gospel be hid, it is hid to them that are lost.
2 CORINTHIANS 4:3 KJV

A question that many believers ask is this: "What about people who never *heard* of Jesus, who never even had a chance to believe? Will *they* go to hell?" A standard response is, "Yes, so that's why you need to preach the Gospel to them." The Bible says, "If our gospel be hid, it is hid to them that are lost" (2 Corinthians 4:3 KJV). By not preaching the gospel, Christians are, in effect, hiding it from those who are perishing.

Some Christians suggest that those who've never heard the Gospel in this life will be given an opportunity to hear it in the *next*. After all, Jesus preached to the formerly disobedient "spirits in prison" (1 Peter 3:19–20 KJV). This answer *seems* reasonable but doesn't find strong support in scripture. Indeed, the Bible seems to exclude it, saying that "each person is destined to die once and after that comes judgment" (Hebrews 9:27 NLT). A more probable scenario is found in Jesus' statement that those who *didn't know* God's will would be punished much less than those who knew the truth but refused to obey it (Luke 12:47–48).

The Bible also indicates that young children who don't know the difference between right and wrong won't be held accountable (Isaiah 7:16). Some also reason that among pagan cultures, the age of accountability would be older. And some Christians point out that although people *before* Christ's day were pagans until they heard the Gospel, God "overlooked people's ignorance" (Acts 17:30 NLT). However, Paul *also* stated that a basic knowledge of good and evil is universal and that at *some* age even the ignorant and unevangelized are accountable. He wrote that pagans "show that they know his law when they instinctively obey it, even without having heard it" (Romans 2:14 NLT). And they also know when they're disobeying.

DISCUSSION QUESTIONS

1. Which possible answer is the most scriptural?
2. Which solution best balances God's love, fairness, and justice?
3. When do children become spiritually accountable?
4. How important is it for Christians to support missionaries?

32.

Is Satan Real?

Be alert and of sober mind. Your enemy the devil prowls around like a roaring lion looking for someone to devour.
1 Peter 5:8 NIV

Yes, Satan exists, and his many names describe the evil he does. The apostle John said, "The great dragon was cast out, that old serpent, called the Devil, and Satan, which deceiveth the whole world" (Revelation 12:9 KJV). The Greek word used for the devil is *diabolos*, which means "accuser," because he is constantly accusing Christians before God (Revelation 12:10). The word used to describe lesser devils, Satan's followers, is *daimon*. These demons are fallen angels (Matthew 25:41). Satan is also called "Beelzebub the prince of the devils" and "the prince of this world" (Matthew 12:24; John 12:31 KJV).

The devil is sometimes called Lucifer because the prophet Isaiah said, "How you are fallen from heaven, O Lucifer, son of the morning!" (Isaiah 14:12 NKJV). Many Christians believe that verses 12–15, part of a description of the fall of the king of Babylon, *also* describe how the devil wanted to be like God and was cast down to hell. In the same way, Ezekiel 28:13–17 is part of a larger description of the king of Tyre, but it's also believed to describe the creation and fall of Satan.

Even if Isaiah and Ezekiel weren't describing Satan, his existence can't be denied. He has been around since the earliest days, deceiving humankind and causing death, destruction, and misery (Genesis 3:1–4; Job 1:1–2:7). Jesus repeatedly cast out demons who were causing all kinds of sickness and diseases (Mark 1:23–27, 32–34). This is the good news: Jesus Christ the Son of God has power over Satan and his demons. And He has given us this same authority, so although we shouldn't be ignorant of Satan's evil workings, we have *power over him* and need not fear him (James 4:7).

DISCUSSION QUESTIONS

1. Was the devil *good* in the very beginning? See Genesis 1:31.
2. Do you believe that Satan is responsible for *all* evil in the world?
3. How much power and authority does Jesus have over Satan?
4. How much authority do *we* have over Satan?

33.

Do Only Good People Go to Heaven?

"No one is good but One, that is, God. But if you want to enter into life, keep the commandments."
MATTHEW 19:17 NKJV

When Jesus told a rich ruler that he needed to obey the commandments to enter into life, the man professed that he'd always kept all of the Ten Commandments faithfully. But when Jesus put him to the test by asking him to give up his riches and follow Him, the man refused. Jesus then explained to His disciples that it was impossible for a rich man to enter the kingdom of God. The disciples asked, "Who then can be saved?" And Jesus replied, "With man this is impossible" (Matthew 19:25–26 NIV). He didn't answer that only *very good* people entered heaven. He said it was impossible for *anyone* to do so. Why? Because *no one* is truly good.

However, Jesus added that with God all things are possible. God can make a way where there is no way. Yet Jesus *had* said, "Keep the commandments"—so which ones then, if not the Ten Commandments? Jesus later stated that the two greatest commands were to love God with all our hearts and to love our neighbor as ourselves (Matthew 22:35–40). The apostle Paul said that those who obey these commands have fulfilled God's law (Romans 13:8; Galatians 5:14).

But remember that it's impossible for even the "righteous," who *try* to keep God's commands, to be saved. So who *can* be saved? Jesus told the religious leaders that tax collectors and prostitutes were entering the kingdom of God ahead of them (Matthew 21:31). How could "sinners" find eternal life before "good" people? Because the sinners repented of their sins and trusted in *Jesus* to save them. John summed up God's law by saying, "And this is his commandment, That we should believe on the name of his Son Jesus Christ, and love one another" (1 John 3:23 KJV). We must believe in Jesus and, by *His* power, live a life of love.

DISCUSSION QUESTIONS

1. Can people inherit heaven by living a good, moral life?
2. Is it fair that repentant sinners are accepted into heaven, but not "good" people?
3. How does God's way keep us honest, humble, and loving?

34.

What Does It Mean to Be "Born Again"?

If anyone is in Christ, he is a new creation; old things have
passed away; behold, all things have become new.
2 Corinthians 5:17 NKJV

What did Jesus mean when He said, "You must be born again" (John 3:7 NKJV)? We've all been born physically, and that event was our *first* birth. But the spirits that live *inside* our bodies needed to receive life as well. Before we were saved, we were like prisoners waiting on death row—as good as dead already. "Sin, when it is full-grown, brings forth death" (James 1:15 NKJV). We needed God to pardon us and remove the death sentence. Our spirits needed to be given life. And God did this. "You. . .He has made alive together with Him, having forgiven you all trespasses" (Colossians 2:13 NKJV).

Jesus said, "That which is born of the flesh is flesh; and that which is born of the Spirit is spirit" (John 3:6 KJV). Being born *again* therefore means being "born of the Spirit." This happens when you believe in Jesus Christ as your Lord and Savior, and God sends the Holy Spirit into your heart. "It is the Spirit who gives life" (John 6:63 NKJV). When the Spirit of Christ enters your heart and gives you eternal life, this is called being born again. Jesus said "again" because this is the *second* birth.

As Paul explained, you become a new creation, a new spiritual being created by God. He has brought you to life, and like a newborn baby, "all things have become new (2 Corinthians 5:17 NKJV). When Jesus' Spirit comes into your life, He redeems you by his power—then *continues* to work in your heart as you mature spiritually. You aren't immediately perfect, but old ways and old sinful habits begin to die out as His Spirit starts to transform you into a new person.

DISCUSSION QUESTIONS

1. What was our former spiritual death sentence?
2. Why is being "born again" called being "born of the Spirit"?
3. What do you think of the concept of spiritual birth?
4. What happens *after* we're born again?

35.

HOW EXACTLY DOES SOMEONE BECOME A CHRISTIAN?

"Believe in the Lord Jesus, and you will be saved."
ACTS 16:31 NIV

The first step toward becoming a Christian is to realize that you're a sinner. The Bible says, "All have sinned" (Romans 3:23 KJV), and it's important that you believe this. Then when you hear the Gospel, the issues come sharply into focus. You realize that there is a heaven and a hell, and that unless you have eternal life, you will suffer for your sins when you die because "the wages of sin is death" (Romans 6:23 KJV). It's also important to know that you can't save yourself.

But the *good* news is that Jesus died on the cross to take the penalty for your sins, and if you depend on Him to save you, He will. At this point, you must sincerely turn away from your selfish ways and pray to God to forgive you. A sense of guilt and regret are *healthy* emotions to experience when you realize that you've done wrong, because that motivates you to repent and seek forgiveness. As Jesus told his listeners, "Repent and believe the good news!" (Mark 1:15 NIV).

Ask God to send the Spirit of Jesus Christ His Son into your heart to give you eternal life, and He will (Galatians 4:6). But you must also know something about who you're putting your trust in. Jesus said, "Believe the good news." But to do this, you must know *what* the good news is. It's important to know the basic facts about Jesus—He was crucified, He died and was buried, and He was raised back to life. Believe these things and you're saved. "If you confess with your mouth the Lord Jesus and believe in your heart that God has raised Him from the dead, you will be saved" (Romans 10:9 NKJV).

DISCUSSION QUESTIONS

1. Why is it important to know that you can't save yourself?
2. What does it mean to repent from your sins?
3. Is "Believe in Jesus and you're saved" the *full* Gospel message?
4. Why must Christians believe that God raised Jesus from the dead?

36.

WHAT IS FAITH?

Faith is the confidence that what we hope for will actually happen; it gives us assurance about things we cannot see.
HEBREWS 11:1 NLT

People often see two different aspects of faith. First, there's the faith they have that God will save them from their sins when they trust in His Son. This is often called "saving faith." Second, they "*have* faith" that God will answer when they pray for something. But faith means believing in the power of God, whether it's faith in Him to save you or faith that He will answer your prayers. "He that spared not his own Son, but delivered him up for us all, how shall he not with him also freely give us all things?" (Romans 8:32 KJV).

Like Abraham, you can be "fully persuaded that God had power to do what he had promised" (Romans 4:21 NIV). This holds true whether you're trusting Him to save your soul in eternity or trusting Him to supply something that you need here and now. If there's a difference, it's that God knows that you genuinely *need* to be saved from hell, whereas you may *not* actually need some of the things you pray for. God knows best, and if He withholds your requests or delays answering them, you must trust that He's doing so with your best interests in mind.

When it comes to your salvation, you can know that "He who promised is faithful" (Hebrews 10:23 NKJV). God has promised to give you eternal life, and

He will be faithful to fulfill that promise. You can be certain that if you believe in Jesus, you'll one day be together with Him in heaven. As the apostle Paul wrote, "I know whom I have believed, and am convinced that he is able" (2 Timothy 1:12 NIV).

DISCUSSION QUESTIONS

1. Faith means trusting someone to keep their word. Is God trustworthy?
2. How does knowing about God's power increase your faith?
3. Why does God sometimes withhold our requests?
4. Are you convinced that He is *able* to save you? Why?

37.

ARE WE SAVED BY FAITH, OR BY FAITH AND GOOD DEEDS?

Your salvation doesn't come from anything you do.
It is God's gift. It is not based on anything you have done.
No one can brag about earning it.
EPHESIANS 2:8–9 NIrV

The Bible says that you are saved by faith in Jesus Christ alone. No good deeds ("works of righteousness") that you do can save you. They don't even contribute a small part to your salvation. When you put your faith in His Son, Jesus, God gives you salvation as a *gift*. You can't *earn* a gift. You simply receive it. If you're given something in exchange for deeds you've done, it's not a gift but a payment. And God has made it clear that salvation cannot be earned.

But you do need *real* faith. It's not enough to simply believe that Jesus existed or that He taught many noble things—or even to try your best to follow His teachings. A mere mental assent that Jesus is God's Son is not enough. So how do you, or anyone else, know that you *have* real faith? By just *saying* that you do? No. As James said, "I will show you my faith by my works" (James 2:18 NKJV). That's how you will clearly see that you have faith. You can't simply attempt to do good deeds on your own, but if you have real faith, the Holy Spirit living in your life will inspire you to do good.

Faith alone saves you, but once Jesus has saved you, you will begin to be "zealous for good works"

(Titus 2:14 NKJV). Your faith will naturally express itself in the loving deeds that you do. Why? The explanation is simple: because faith expresses itself through love (Galatians 5:6). The reason for this is that God Himself *is* love, and when His Spirit comes into your heart and lives inside you, He expresses His presence by motivating you to do good, loving deeds.

DISCUSSION QUESTIONS

1. What is the difference between receiving a gift and earning something?
2. What is a sure proof that you have real faith?
3. Why is love the dynamic force behind faith?
4. Is love always a warm feeling, or sometimes just obedience?

38.

How Can Jesus Live inside My Heart?

*And because you are sons, God has sent forth the Spirit
of His Son into your hearts.*

GALATIANS 4:6 NKJV

God wanted to send the Spirit of His Son into our
hearts because He knew that we needed to be empowered to be *able* to live the Christian life. Revelation
3:20 says that Jesus is standing at the door and knocking, and if we open the door, He will enter our lives.
Even though Christ was talking to the already saved in
this passage, it's a good picture of what happens when
He *first* comes into our hearts as well.

We know that Jesus lives in our hearts because the
Bible tells us that "those who do not have the Spirit of
Christ living in them do not belong to him" (Romans
8:9 NLT). So we must *have* the Spirit of Christ living
in us to be saved. Paul tells us that Christ dwells in our
hearts through faith, so it is our faith, our believing in
Him, that initiates this experience (Ephesians 3:17).
When we cry out to God to forgive our sins and to give
us eternal life, He sends the Spirit of His Son into our
hearts—the core of our beings.

Jesus is now seated at the right hand of His Father
in heaven, so how can He also be all over the entire
world dwelling in the hearts of hundreds of millions
of believers? Very likely the answer is that just as Jesus
is *one* with God the Father, so he's *one* with the Holy
Spirit—and we know that the Holy Spirit lives inside

us as well. God "hath given us of his Spirit" (1 John 4:13 KJV). God has also promised that His Holy Spirit is the guarantee (God's seal stamped on us) that we will inherit eternal life (Ephesians 1:13–14).

DISCUSSION QUESTIONS

1. Does Christ actually dwell in us, or is that just a metaphor?
2. Why does God send the Holy Spirit into our hearts?
3. Do you *feel* like Jesus is living inside you? Why or why not?
4. How does Jesus' Spirit help you live a Christian life?

39.

WILL GOD FORGIVE ME FOR SINNING AFTER I'M SAVED?

If we confess our sins, he is faithful and just and will forgive us our sins and purify us from all unrighteousness.
1 JOHN 1:9 NIV

Some Christians teach that after a person is saved, they become completely sinless and perfect. First John 3:9 is often used to support this doctrine: "Whoever has been born of God does not sin" (NKJV). If anyone *does* sin—even in tiny ways—they believe that this proves they were never saved to begin with. They also note that Jesus told us to be "perfect" just as God is perfect (Matthew 5:48). However, it should be pointed out that the Greek word translated here as "perfect" means "complete," not sinless.

But most Christians believe that a doctrine of complete sinlessness is unrealistic and, more importantly, goes against the overwhelming evidence of scripture. They point out that God has declared that our righteousness before Him is a divine gift *imputed* to us (credited to our account) because of our faith in Jesus Christ—even though we are weak, imperfect people (Romans 4:21–25). When God looks at us, He doesn't see our *lack* of righteousness, but the righteousness of Christ whose blood covers our sins.

Jesus told His disciples to forgive a brother who kept on sinning and sinning against them (Matthew 18:21–22), evidence that believers aren't exempt from sin. John makes this plain when he writes, "These things I write to you, so that you may not sin. And if anyone sins, we have an Advocate with the Father, Jesus Christ" (1 John 2:1 NKJV). Here John advised Christians to do their best to obey God and *not* to sin, but stated that if they *did* sin, to repent and turn to God for forgiveness—and yes, God would forgive them.

"Well then, should we keep on sinning so that God can show us more and more of his wonderful grace? Of course not!" (Romans 6:1–2 NLT).

DISCUSSION QUESTIONS

1. Do you believe Christians should be perfect? How?
2. What does it mean that righteousness is "imputed" to us?
3. Will God forgive you for sinning after you're saved?
4. What happens if you don't repent and ask for forgiveness?

40.

CAN TRUE CHRISTIANS "LOSE" THEIR SALVATION?

"All that the Father gives Me will come to Me,
and the one who comes to Me I will by no means cast out."
JOHN 6:37 NKJV

Christians have two different views on whether it is possible to lose your salvation. We will examine them both. What follows is not a comprehensive study of the subject, but merely the basic points.

Some believe that while people cannot "lose" their salvation by accident or because of sins that they repent of, they can lose faith or willfully renounce salvation and turn from it—through continual evil behavior. The Bible *does* say that if we deliberately continue to sin after we have received knowledge of the truth, there is no longer any sacrifice to cover these sins (Hebrews 10:26). And Hebrews 10:32 seems to be talking about Christians. Also, Paul said in 1 Corinthians 9:27 that he exercised self-control so he wouldn't become a castaway. This is why some people teach that we must *remain faithful* to Christ to be saved.

Other Christians maintain that the Bible declares that we have "eternal security." They agree that willful, sinful behavior grieves God's Spirit who lives in our hearts (Ephesians 4:30). But because Jesus promised in Hebrews 13:5 that He would never leave us, they don't believe that the Spirit then *leaves* us. Paul also said that *nothing* could separate him from the love of

God in Jesus Christ (Romans 8:38–39). He also stated that no matter how many of a Christian's sinful deeds are burned at the Judgment, "he himself will be saved" (1 Corinthians 3:11–15 NKJV). They're saved even if they later become "faithless" (2 Timothy 2:13 NKJV).

Christians who believe in eternal security point out that if God requires *our* help to keep us saved, then we're no longer saved by grace alone, but also by good works—which is unscriptural (Romans 11:6). There are, of course, counterarguments for each point made here.

DISCUSSION QUESTIONS

1. What do you believe on this issue? Why?
2. How do you explain the verses Christians who believe differently than you quote?
3. Is being faithful to Christ a "works" salvation?
4. What sins might cause people to "lose" their salvation?

41.

DOES GOD JUDGE OR PUNISH US FOR SINNING?

*"Those whom I love I rebuke and discipline.
So be earnest and repent."*
REVELATION 3:19 NIV

If you were born again and believe in Jesus Christ, you're now a son or daughter of God. You're no longer destined to be condemned like the rest of the world, nor will you face God's judgment, but you've passed from death to life (John 5:24). However, for that very reason, *because* you're now God's child and He's concerned about your behavior, He *will* discipline you when you sin. The fact that God disciplines you is proof that He loves you deeply. He cares enough about you to correct you. Pause right now and take the time to read Hebrews 12:5–11 to understand God's loving correction.

These verses from Hebrews offer comfort, because God's rebukes can unsettle us and His discipline can seem hard. When stricken with sicknesses, financial setbacks, or accidents, we sometimes wonder if God has abandoned us. We might mistake His chastening as the angry judgment of God—even though we know we've repented of our sins. In fact, even when we *recognize* God's discipline for what it is, and realize that its intent is to bring forth *good* in our lives, it can still be very hard to endure.

But as Job said, "Consider the joy of those corrected by God!" (Job 5:17 NLT) Joy? It may not seem like it at the time. We don't enjoy being disciplined. It's painful, but after we've learned from it, we have peace because we start living the right way again (Hebrews 12:11). God says, "Be earnest and repent." When you repent, you *stop* doing things that displease God or that hurt yourself and others. You start living life as you're supposed to. And *that* gives you peace and joy.

DISCUSSION QUESTIONS

1. What are your thoughts on Hebrews 12:5–11?
2. Can you compare God's chastisement to disciplining a child?
3. Has God ever disciplined you to bring you into line? How?
4. Have you confused God's correction for judgment?

42.

WHY SHOULD I OBEY GOD?

*"Those who accept my commandments and obey them
are the ones who love me."*
JOHN 14:21 NLT

Being saved isn't just a one-time experience that lets
you avoid hell. It means being born into a new life
and is the beginning of a relationship with God and
His Son Jesus Christ. You're not saved just so you can
walk streets of gold. Remember, heaven is where *God*
dwells, and the main reason for being there is to be
with Him—forever. Relationships are built on love,
and we prove that we love God by obeying Him.

Some may ask, "Once I'm saved, why should I
sacrifice and deny myself life's little pleasures? If I'm
going to heaven whether I obey God or not, why
bother?" Besides the fact that true Christians desire to
please God, He has given us other motivations. Each
of us must one day appear before the judgment seat
of Christ to account for every word we've ever spoken and every deed we've ever done—whether good
or bad (2 Corinthians 5:10). This judgment isn't to
determine whether we go to heaven. That was already
settled when we accepted Jesus. Rather, this is when
we're greatly rewarded for our obedience but suffer loss
for all our sins and disobedience.

In 1 Corinthians 3:10–15, Paul compares our
rewards in heaven to building a glorious house. The
foundation of our salvation is Jesus Christ Himself, but

how we live life here on earth determines what our heavenly house will be. If we build on the foundation with gold, silver, or costly stones (good deeds and obedience), when the fire of God tests it, our house will remain standing, unscathed. However, if we build with wood, hay, or straw (selfish deeds and disobedience), the fire shall utterly consume it. We'll still have our foundation (salvation) but no house. It's to our benefit to live lives that God can reward.

DISCUSSION QUESTIONS

1. How is our obedience the result of a loving relationship?
2. What happens at the judgment seat of Christ?
3. What kind of good deeds and obedient acts will be rewarded?
4. What kind of misdeeds and disobedient acts will be burned?
5. How would the lack of any reward be a terrible loss?

43.

Are Christians Supposed to Be Happy All the Time?

In all this you greatly rejoice, though now for a little while you may have had to suffer grief in all kinds of trials.
1 Peter 1:6 NIV

An overly enthusiastic Sunday school song repeats the phrase "I'm happy all the time!" And many Christians have the impression that since Jesus saved them, they *should* be happy all the time. After all, doesn't the Bible say in Psalm 144 (NLT) that "joyful indeed are those whose God is the Lord"? And isn't happiness a *choice*? Can't everyone simply decide to be happy? Many Christians wonder what's wrong when they're sad, stressed out, or mourning great losses. They feel guilty when they're downcast and sometimes even refuse to grieve. While maintaining a positive attitude is great, expecting to be happy *all* the time is neither healthy nor realistic.

Before his statement above, Peter had just reminded his readers that God had chosen them, saved them, and given them hope through a new spiritual birth. Not only that, but God had cleansed them and made them holy by His Spirit. Peter had then described how an inheritance that would never fade away was being reserved for them in heaven. Furthermore, they were being shielded by God's power, through faith, until that day. That's what he meant when he said, "In *all this* you greatly rejoice."

Yes, because of our future glorious hope, we *can* rejoice even through our tears. We can rejoice despite the grief we're suffering from temptations, sicknesses, or persecution. None of these things are pleasant. In fact, Jesus warned that we'd sometimes be sad, saying, "Blessed are they that mourn." He then said that the *reason* we're blessed is because we "shall be comforted" *one day* (Matthew 5:4 KJV). We can expect to cry at times now, but one day God will wipe away our tears (Revelation 7:17). For all these reasons—*despite* our present sorrows—we can "rejoice with joy inexpressible" (1 Peter 1:8 NKJV).

DISCUSSION QUESTIONS

1. Is it realistic to expect to be happy all the time?
2. Is happiness *usually* a choice, or *always*?
3. How can we experience joy even when we're sad or miserable?
4. Does thinking about heaven give you joy?

44.

What If Something Just Feels Right?

The heart is deceitful above all things and beyond cure.
Who can understand it?
JEREMIAH 17:9 NIV

Our emotions are a gift from God. Life without emotions would be bland and colorless. As humans we experience a broad spectrum of feelings: We *grieve* a loved one's passing. We *rejoice* in the birth of a child. We *triumph* in our successes. Most importantly, we can experience the "joy" of salvation (Psalm 51:12) and "the peace of God, which surpasses all understanding" (Philippians 4:7 NKJV). Emotions are spectacular. They make us feel alive, and they can be one of God's greatest blessings on our lives. But God also warns us that our feelings can betray us. We have to be aware of our emotions and make sure that they don't govern our decision-making process.

Popular culture tells us that right and wrong are open for interpretation—that we should do whatever *feels* good. But God has given us a better way. As Christians we must remember that we live in a fallen world, and sin permeates our culture. We can't look within ourselves for a moral compass because sin is ingrained in our nature. That's why God left us with an instruction manual—the Bible. In the same way that parents provide guidance for their short-sighted children, our heavenly Father has outlined the good behavior He expects of us.

God has also given us "the mind of Christ" (1 Corinthians 2:16 KJV). He wants us to think like Him and nurture our personal integrity by meditating on His Word and living according to His laws. By doing this, we can avoid temptation and live prosperous and successful lives (Joshua 1:8). God isn't providing us with a magical formula that will make us rich and famous. But if we live according to the wisdom of the scriptures instead of being ruled by our emotions, He will bless us with an abundant life.

DISCUSSION QUESTIONS

1. Why did God give us emotions?
2. How can our feelings mislead us?
3. How do we determine "good" emotions from "bad" emotions?

45.

WHY IS BEING "WORLDLY" A BAD THING?

Do not love the world or the things in the world. If anyone loves the world, the love of the Father is not in him.
1 JOHN 2:15 NKJV

Some people are surprised to hear that there's anything wrong with being worldly. After all, according to the dictionary, *worldly* means "experienced in life" or "sophisticated." Does the Bible imply that it's preferable to be *in*experienced and *un*sophisticated? Is being naive a virtue? No. When the Bible speaks against being worldly, it's referring to someone who is engrossed in temporal affairs, especially the pursuit of wealth and pleasure. We all need a certain amount of money and creature comforts, but to be obsessed with them is wrong. When we love the things of this world *too* much, it displaces our love for God.

The Bible further defines worldliness in an even darker light, calling it "the lust of the flesh, and the lust of the eyes, and the pride of life" (1 John 2:16 KJV). Such motivations don't lead us to make the right choices or to live godly lives. The lust of the flesh, for example, consists of "ungodliness and worldly passions" (Titus 2:12 NIV), whereas Christians are to live godly lives and exercise self-control. The lust of the eyes is any kind of lust or covetousness, and the tenth commandment warns us not to covet anything that belongs to someone else. And from cover to cover, the Bible speaks against pride.

This doesn't mean that some Christians don't have worldly inclinations or that they *never* become overly focused on material things. What it *does* mean, however, is that "people who are still worldly [are] mere infants in Christ" (1 Corinthians 3:1 NIV). And we need to grow up and become more spiritual. We learn how to follow God by reading the Bible, and Jesus warned that caring too much about this world chokes out God's Word in our lives (Matthew 13:22).

DISCUSSION QUESTIONS

1. Is it wrong to be experienced in life and sophisticated?
2. What do you think "love not the world" means?
3. Why are lust and pride such corrupting sins?
4. How does being worldly affect our relationship with God?

46.

IS GOD IN CONTROL OF EVERYTHING THAT HAPPENS?

"I have set before you life and death, blessing and cursing; therefore choose life, that both you and your descendants may live."
DEUTERONOMY 30:19 NKJV

Many Christians believe that since God is omnipotent and omniscient, that He preordained all things before time began and they happen now because He *willed* them to happen. Other Christians argue that this view is fatalistic and that God has left a great deal up to our concern—free will and choice.

Our view on this issue definitely influences important life decisions. For example, Christians who believe that God planned their future mate before time began are likely to wait for that one, preordained person to come along (Genesis 24:13–15). In contrast, Christians who believe in free choice generally believe that they may marry whomever they wish, so long as that person is a Christian (1 Corinthians 7:39).

When it comes to salvation, the two main views are Calvinism, which stresses God's sovereignty (He alone chooses who will be saved) and Arminianism, which stresses humanity's free will (God has left it to us whether we accept His offer of grace or not). Calvinism emphasizes "God's election," which means God's choice in the matter. Paul wrote, "So then it is not of him who wills. . .but of God who shows mercy" (Romans 9:16 NKJV). Many other verses are also quoted to support this view. See Romans 8:29–30; 9:11–12; 11:5–7.

Other Christians believe that God has left it up to us to choose or reject Him. In the Bible, God repeatedly tells people to "choose. . .whom you will serve" (Joshua 24:15 NLT). Although it is not God's will that *anyone* perish (Matthew 18:14), many do reject God. Even in the famous chapter on "election," Paul mentions that though some people are objects of God's wrath, He has great patience toward them (Romans 9:22). As Romans 2:4 explains, the *purpose* of God's great patience is for these vessels of wrath to repent and be saved.

DISCUSSION QUESTIONS

1. Which doctrinal position do you believe is right?
2. Do you need to study the subject more before you decide?
3. How do your views on God's will affect your life choices?

47.

WHY DOES GOD ALLOW SO MUCH SUFFERING IN THE WORLD?

The heaven, even the heavens, are the LORD's;
but the earth He has given to the children of men.
PSALM 115:16 NKJV

Is God in direct control of every disaster that happens on earth? Does *every* earthquake, volcanic eruption, tsunami, and typhoid outbreak happen as a result of divine intervention? For Christians who believe that God allows suffering, the reason is one of the following: (a) to judge sin in the world; (b) to show by His power that He is God; or (c) to bring discipline to cause people to repent and turn to Him.

Others believe that while God is certainly able to bring good out of disasters (Romans 8:28), most are a consequence of the natural physical laws God set in motion during Creation. Just as gravity works without His continual intervention, they say that we shouldn't interpret every earthquake as an act of God—although He's indeed capable of causing one.

Many times in the Old Testament, God *was* described as the one who brought disaster on His disobedient people—whether droughts, earthquakes, swarms of locusts, or plagues. But some of the worst droughts and famines are mentioned simply as historical events with no indication that they were judgments handed down by God (Genesis 12:10; 26:1). Disasters and calamities also give God's people an opportunity to demonstrate their love. When the Christians in Antioch learned that a famine would happen, the Bible doesn't tell us whether they theorized *why* it was happening—but it *does* tell us that they sent relief money (Acts 11:27–30).

Much suffering in the world today is a result of the hatred and greed of humankind—war, economic depressions, pollution, and oppression. God promises that He will one day step in and stop all suffering, but until that day, "if you see the poor oppressed in a district, and justice and rights denied, do not be surprised" (Ecclesiastes 5:8 NIV).

DISCUSSION QUESTIONS

1. Do you believe that God *directly* causes all natural disasters?
2. What do you believe is His purpose in this?
3. How does God want us to react when disasters happen?
4. How much suffering do *people* cause in this world?

48.

WHY DOES GOD ALLOW GOOD PEOPLE TO SUFFER?

Don't be surprised by the painful suffering you are going through. . . . Be joyful that you are taking part in Christ's sufferings.
1 PETER 4:12–13 NIrV

Often, the very fact that we're Christians is enough to bring suffering on us. Antagonistic people may insult and persecute us. They may spread rumors about us or do spiteful things to make our lives difficult (2 Timothy 3:12). When the first Christians were being persecuted, Peter told them not to wonder what strange thing was happening. After all, Jesus had said, "If they persecuted Me, they will also persecute you" (John 15:20 NKJV). When we follow in Jesus' footsteps, those who hate Him will hate us also. He said to rejoice when that happens, because God will greatly reward us in heaven as a result (Matthew 5:11–12).

Of course, not all problems that Christians encounter are a result of persecution. God also allows us to suffer delays, losses, and sicknesses. But once again, we are told that we should rejoice when these things happen. Why should problems and setbacks be a cause for joy? Because, Paul says that we know that God is allowing them to strengthen us, teach us patience, and develop endurance (Romans 5:3). "The Lord tests our hearts" (Proverbs 17:3 NIrV) to bring our flaws to our attention and to help us become better people.

God sometimes causes us to suffer when we're disobedient so we'll come back in line and begin to obey Him again. Once more we are told to look on the positive side and, like the psalmist, to say, "It is good for me that I have been afflicted, that I may learn Your statutes" (Psalm 119:71 NKJV). When this happens, God is not *judging* us for our sin. Rather, His loving chastisements are proof that we are His beloved sons and daughters, and that He cares for us (Hebrews 12:5–11).

DISCUSSION QUESTIONS

1. Which three kinds of suffering should cause us to rejoice?
2. How can unselfish choices also make our lives harder?
3. What good have *you* experienced through setbacks and problems?
4. Have you ever experienced God's loving correction?

49.

DOES GOD TRULY CARE ABOUT ME?

*Behold what manner of love the Father has bestowed
on us, that we should be called children of God!*
1 JOHN 3:1 NKJV

We know that God is a loving God and everything
He allows to happen is for a good purpose. We also
know that when seemingly evil things happen, He can
use them to bring about good (Romans 8:28). We can
even understand that God isn't judging us in anger,
but that He is correcting us as a loving Father. In spite
of our knowledge of God's love for us, when we suffer prolonged sicknesses or painful estrangements or
endure financial hardships—we can seriously doubt
that God actually cares.

In the Psalms, David was once so emotionally over-
whelmed that he cried out, "My God, my God, why
have you forsaken me?" (Psalm 22:1 NIV). Sometimes
it literally feels like God *has* forsaken us. Even though
He *hasn't*, the experience can be excruciating. This is
especially true when we've brought trouble on ourselves through our own mistakes.

At such times, we must remind ourselves of the
basics—our heavenly Father loves us so much that
He sent His Son to die for our sins so we could have
eternal life. We often become so engrossed in this life
that heaven can seem somewhat distant and irrelevant.
But in times of severe testing, it gives us hope to know
that God—who cannot lie—has promised us eternal

life. "This hope we have as an anchor of the soul, both sure and steadfast" (Hebrews 6:19 NKJV).

And even though God may not immediately change our circumstances and relieve our suffering, He feels deeply what we're going through. "In all their suffering he also suffered" (Isaiah 63:9 NLT). Remember, God's Son Jesus lived as a man on earth and can *identify* with our suffering. He is "touched with the feeling of our infirmities" (Hebrews 4:15 KJV). God loves us and He feels what we're going through—He cares.

DISCUSSION QUESTIONS

1. Have you had times when you felt God *didn't* care?
2. How comforting is the hope of eternal life to you?
3. What do you think the expression "anchor of the soul" means?
4. How deeply do you think God feels *your* pain?

50.

WILL GOD SOLVE ALL MY PROBLEMS?

The righteous person may have many troubles,
but the LORD delivers him from them all.
PSALM 34:19 NIV

In Deuteronomy 28:1–14, Moses gave a long list of financial and material blessings that God would give His people if they, as a nation, faithfully obeyed His Law. Christians today still claim these promises of problem-free material blessings for their own lives. They realize, of course, that trouble is bound to come their way, but they believe that God will protect them from it all. After all, David said, "The righteous cry out, and the LORD hears, and delivers them out of all their troubles" (Psalm 34:17 NKJV). Some very positive-thinking Christians believe that this means if they love God and live righteously, that he's literally *obliged* to keep all trouble out of their lives—or to quickly resolve it.

But this verse isn't saying our lives will always be easy. In fact, only two verses later the Bible says that "The righteous person may have *many* troubles" (Psalm 34:19 NIV). As a Christian, you can expect to experience many setbacks, hardships, and problems. That is a promise. "We must suffer many hardships to enter the Kingdom of God" (Acts 14:22 NLT). Even Jesus told us, "In the world you will have tribulation" (John 16:33 NKJV).

It may take time, and you may have to endure some troubles for a while, but God will eventually save you from all of them. You may have to endure some problems, such as long-term illnesses or less than desirable finances much of your life, and you may not be completely free from them until you enter into God's presence in heaven. Remember, God can and does bless His children materially, but as Christians our primary focus must *not* be on financial abundance. Nor should we expect our lives to be problem-free.

DISCUSSION QUESTIONS

1. Has God promised Christians abundant material blessings?
2. Do you believe that God will solve all your problems?
3. How many troubles have you gone through as a Christian?
4. How quickly has God promised to deliver you from them?

51.

WHY SHOULD I PRAY IF GOD KNOWS EVERYTHING ALREADY?

"When you pray, do not use vain repetitions. . . .
For your Father knows the things you have
need of before you ask Him."
MATTHEW 6:7–8 NKJV

God is *omniscient*, which means all-knowing. He knows the number of hairs on your head, and even what every sparrow on earth is doing at any given moment (Luke 12:6–7). Such omniscience may be incomprehensible to us, but that's precisely the point: God is God and is too vast for our minds to comprehend.

Jesus was addressing God's omniscience when He said not to use "vain repetitions" like the pagans did when they prayed. They thought that the *longer* they prayed, the more likely it was that their gods would *finally* hear them. They also had to make sure that their uninformed gods knew what they needed. When we state our requests simply and don't needlessly repeat ourselves, we're acknowledging that God is all-wise and *already* knows what we need. So why should we bother to pray if God already knows exactly what we need?

God is not a distant, uncaring deity. He is our loving Father. We are His children and have a personal relationship with Him. That's why He wants us to speak to Him with trust. Prayer is not some formal mumbo jumbo, but sincere communication with a loving God—so we can talk to Him from our hearts.

Although God knows what we require, He wants *us* to fully realize our needs as well and to be aware that He alone has the power to supply what we need. Prayer is a way of acknowledging *our* inability and limitations and *God's* ability and unlimited power. When we do this, we admit our dependence on Him. We're also verbalizing that He is God, which is a form of worship. So talk to God today. He says, "Call to Me, and I will answer you" (Jeremiah 33:3 NKJV).

DISCUSSION QUESTIONS

1. How does our relationship with God affect *how* we talk to Him?
2. How is acknowledging God's power a form of worship?
3. If *all* your needs were fully met, would you still pray?

52.

WHY DO WE HAVE TO KEEP PRAYING FOR THE SAME THING?

"Keep on asking, and you will receive what you ask for. Keep on seeking, and you will find."
MATTHEW 7:7 NLT

In Matthew 6:7 (KJV), Jesus told us not to use "vain repetitions" when we pray. Yet only a few verses later He advised, "Keep on asking and it will be given you." (This verse is usually translated to read, "*Ask* and it will be given you," but the original Greek means "Keep on asking.") And that is precisely what people in the Bible did. Elijah prayed for rain *seven* times (1 Kings 18:42–44). And Jesus, when He was praying in the Garden of Gethsemane, prayed *three* times "saying the same words" (Matthew 26:44 NKJV).

There's no contradiction, however. Their prayers were repeated, but they weren't "vain" (empty, useless) repetitions. They were desperate, heartfelt cries to God. So yes, there are definitely times when we *need* to pray repeatedly for the same thing. Part of the reason for this is that it shows that we care deeply for the person or the need that we're praying for. And it's a biblical command to pray persistently: "They will pray day and night, continually. Take no rest, all you who pray to the LORD. Give the LORD no rest until he completes his work" (Isaiah 62:6–7 NLT).

We also need to pray without ceasing because Satan fiercely fights God's will. This is often the reason we have to pray so much and wait so long for answers to our prayers. The prophet Daniel once prayed for twenty-one days before an angel finally arrived with the answer. The angel told Daniel that his prayers had been heard from the first day but that a demon had fought him to prevent him from getting through with the answer (Daniel 10:1–13). So "be alert and always keep on praying for all the Lord's people" (Ephesians 6:18 NIV).

DISCUSSION QUESTIONS

1. Are *all* repeated prayers "vain repetition"? Why or why not?
2. How do continual prayers show our concern?
3. Why is it important to pray and not stop praying?
4. What have you been praying about for months— or years?

53.

Does God Always Answer Prayer?

*And ye shall seek me, and find me,
when ye shall search for me with all your heart.*
JEREMIAH 29:13 KJV

A Christian proverb says: "God *always* answers prayer. Sometimes His answer is yes, other times His answer is no, and sometimes His answer is wait." This is true to a certain extent, but there is more. As question 52 points out, sometimes the answer is "Yes, but don't stop praying yet."

Also there are times when God *doesn't* answer prayer. He may not answer because we haven't prayed wholeheartedly. We are told to seek the Lord with all our heart and cry out desperately for His help. We are told to stir ourselves up to take hold of God (Isaiah 64:7). We are to be like Jacob wrestling the angel of the Lord, *refusing* to let go until He blesses us (Genesis 32:24–29). But if we *don't* pray wholeheartedly when we should, God won't answer. Whereas if we *do* pray fervently, He will respond powerfully. "The earnest prayer of a righteous person has great power and produces wonderful results" (James 5:16 NLT).

The presence of sin in our lives might also prevent God from answering our prayers. David noted, "If I had not confessed the sin in my heart, the Lord would not have listened" (Psalm 66:18 NLT). Unconfessed sins create a disconnection between us and God. If our relationship is broken, He won't listen—at least not with an intent to answer (Isaiah 59:1–2). But sometimes we automatically assume that people's prayers aren't answered because they've sinned. This *may* be the case, or it may *not* be. It's not for us to judge.

If we're just speaking words and we lack the faith that God can answer our prayers, He may choose not to. Whereas, if we pray with faith, God will answer our prayers (Mark 11:24; James 1:6–7).

DISCUSSION QUESTIONS

1. Do you believe that God *always* answers prayer? Why?
2. What happens when we pray with wrong motives? See James 4:3.
3. Is sin *often* the reason for unanswered prayer?
4. Have you had an answer to wholehearted prayer?

54.

WHY ARE SO MANY CHRISTIANS HYPOCRITES?

*"But why do you call Me 'Lord, Lord,'
and not do the things which I say?"*
LUKE 6:46 NKJV

Many people who call themselves Christians are, in
fact, hypocrites. Even genuine Christians are guilty of
minor acts of hypocrisy at some point. But being a
hypocrite is a serious charge, so we should be cautious
about accusing people or else we'll be guilty of judging others—something Jesus warned against (Matthew
7:1–2). By definition, hypocrites are people who deliberately put on a show of goodness when they're fully
aware that they're not. The Greek word *hypokrites* that
Jesus used means "an actor in a play." A hypocrite is
acting at living as a Christian—sometimes putting on a
convincing performance, too—but they know they're
not really following Christ.

Jesus' definition of a hypocrite was simple. He said
that "they say, and do not do" (Matthew 23:3 NKJV).
You can read Christ's denunciation of the scribes and
Pharisees in Matthew 23, where He gives clear-cut
examples of their evil actions, which contradicted their
pious prayers and proclamations of faith. Even their
giving to God was in stark contrast to their unjust
treatment of the poor and vulnerable during the week.
Jesus said that at the Final Judgment He would ask
such people, "Why do you call me 'Lord, Lord,' and
do not do what I say?" (Luke 6:46 NIV). And what

did Jesus say we should do? Love God with all our hearts and to love others as much as we love ourselves (Matthew 22:36–39).

While we're often tempted to judge hypocrisy in *other* people's lives, it's best that we leave the judging to Jesus, the righteous Judge. It's far more profitable for us to examine the areas in *our* lives where we're disobeying God—where we "say, and do not do."

DISCUSSION QUESTIONS

1. What are the two definitions of a hypocrite?
2. How can we be mistaken when judging others' hypocrisy?
3. Can a genuine Christian be a hypocrite? Why or why not?
4. What kinds of hypocrisy do we need to guard against?

55.

ARE CHRISTIANS INTOLERANT?

Ye that love the LORD, hate evil.
PSALM 97:10 KJV

The New Testament gives us clear guidelines on how to live our lives. It outlines honest business ethics, forbids theft and pilfering, warns against wild partying and drunkenness, defines sexual morality, forbids materialism and covetousness, and is clear about the sanctity of life. The world around us may not live according to the Bible's standards, but the Lord says to *us*, "Come out from them and be separate" (2 Corinthians 6:17 NIV). We are not to engage in their sins.

Although Paul wrote that believers were not to tolerate sin or keep company with immoral people, he was careful to point out that he meant those who called themselves *Christians* yet were immoral. He didn't mean for us to withdraw from the world (1 Corinthians 5:9–12). After all, a great many people around us aren't living according to Christian morals in one way or another.

Many people are content to let Christians live their faith so long as they don't attempt to impose their values on *them*—or on society at large. Often this is when Christians are accused of being intolerant and "holier than thou." Much of the sharpest criticism comes from those who were raised in Christian homes, whose parents tried to instill biblical values in them. These children, if they later rebel, often become outspoken critics of what they consider confining and intolerant Christian teachings.

We can't help what our critics think about our faith, and we can't agree with them just for the sake of peace, but we blunt a great deal of their criticism when we present our views gently and patiently—and not in argumentative ways (2 Timothy 2:24). We must speak the truth, yes, but we should speak it in love (Ephesians 4:15). Because only God can change people's lives.

DISCUSSION QUESTIONS

1. Are many Christians actually intolerant? Why?
2. *Should* we tolerate everything that happens in society?
3. How effective is legislating or imposing righteousness?
4. What should our attitude be when we're accused of intolerance?

56.

WHAT DOES GOD THINK IF
I EXPERIENCE DOUBT?

The apostles said to the Lord, "Increase our faith!"
LUKE 17:5 NIV

Some doubt is good. You *should* have reservations when someone urges you to invest but the deal seems too good to be true. You *should* be skeptical when people teach doctrines contrary to the Gospel. The Bible says that only the simpleminded believe *every* word (Proverbs 14:15).

The Christian faith, however, is "true and reasonable" (Acts 26:25 NIV). The accounts of Jesus' life were carefully written down by eyewitnesses and record the many miracles that He performed, as well as listing infallible proofs that He was raised from the dead (Acts 1:3). And God intended that these records inspire our faith in Jesus. John stated that these things were written "so that you may believe" (John 20:31 NIRV).

Sometimes during severe testing or when faced with perplexing questions, we feel like the man who cried out to Jesus, "Lord, I believe; help my unbelief!" (Mark 9:24 NKJV). God is perfectly able to do a miracle and increase our faith, but more often than not He requires *our* participation. Just as we eat physical food in order to grow and have strength, so we must read God's Word to grow in spiritual strength. Our faith increases when we study and meditate on the scriptures, especially the teachings of Christ in the

New Testament (Romans 10:17).

Faith is important for two reasons: First, we're saved by faith. Second, our ongoing relationship with God depends on how much we trust Him. For example, we must have faith when we pray in order to receive answers (Hebrews 11:6). If your faith is weak or you're experiencing doubt in certain areas, don't put up with it! Study God's Word, seek out answers, and pray for the Lord to increase your faith.

DISCUSSION QUESTIONS

1. How can being skeptical sometimes be a *good* thing?
2. When is doubt unreasonable and irrational? What causes this?
3. Why is it hard to relate to God if you don't trust Him?
4. What are two good ways to increase your faith?

57

Does the Bible Tell Us How to Overcome Fear?

Whenever I am afraid, I will trust in You.
Psalm 56:3 NKJV

Fear is a natural human emotion. When we're in danger, or even *think* we're threatened, we become uneasy. We believe that something bad is about to happen. This leads to worry and anxiety, which can develop into outright fear. We feel fear when faced with physical danger or even an uncertain future. But fear can also have positive results. It can cause us to avoid danger and take action to prevent loss. Yet more often than not, fear has a paralyzing effect or causes us to make impulsive, unwise decisions.

We all experience fear, but the question is how we react. Do we simply let it take over, or like David, do we determine that *when* we're afraid, we'll trust God? (Psalm 56:3). To trust in God during impending disaster, we have to be convinced that he's powerful enough to protect us. We must also believe that he's *with* us and that He *cares* enough to help us. David believed this, which is why he could confidently declare, "I will fear no evil; for You are with me" (Psalm 23:4 NKJV).

If we're convinced that God is both powerful enough *and* cares enough to help us, then no matter how threatening the circumstances are—no matter how hopeless our situation—we're able to say, "I will trust, and not be afraid" (Isaiah 12:2 KJV). Fear sweeps in when we stop believing (Mark 4:40), so we must make a conscious decision to trust God. This often takes a real effort of will. At first, our trust may seem illogical in the face of the threat. But if we have faith, the emotional storm inside will begin to settle, and peace will displace fear. And eventually the storm *around* us will calm as well.

DISCUSSION QUESTIONS

1. What negative effects do fear and worry have on *you*?
2. Have you ever overcome fear by trusting God? Describe it.
3. Why did David declare that he would fear *no* evil?
4. Which of the verses quoted above encourages you the most?

58.

WHY SHOULD I ATTEND CHURCH?

Let us not neglect our meeting together, as some people do,
but encourage one another.
HEBREWS 10:25 NLT

Jesus said that the Church (not a building, but the assembly of believers) is His body, and He is our head (1 Corinthians 12:12–27; Ephesians 4:15–16). Just as a body obeys its head, we are to follow Christ and work together. Just as our hand automatically goes out to touch any part of our body that experiences pain, we are also to care for other members of Christ's body. If fellow Christians are hurting or discouraged, we should reach out to them. We should, as the Bible says, rejoice with those who rejoice and weep with those who weep (Romans 12:15).

Being faithful to attend a church building every Sunday (or Saturday), just because that's what we're "supposed" to do, is not the point. Christians are to love other believers and desire to be with them—to hear the Word of God together, to worship together, to pray for one another, and to encourage each other. Yes, we should worship God alone and privately, but it's good for Christians to *gather* for fellowship. Jesus promised that when even a few of us are together in His name, he's present in the midst of us (Matthew 18:20). King David said, "I went with them to the house of God, with the voice of joy and praise, with a multitude that kept holyday" (Psalm 42:4 KJV).

Church is not just something man thought up—it's God's idea. Wherever Paul traveled preaching the Gospel and winning people to Christ, he established churches, assemblies of believers. The first Christians met regularly (Acts 2:42; 20:7; 1 Corinthians 16:3) to listen to the Word being read and preached, to worship God together, and to give offerings. We should, too.

DISCUSSION QUESTIONS

1. Why should Christians meet together regularly?
2. Why do we sometimes find "church attendance" boring?
3. Why is solitary prayer and worship not enough?
4. Do you feel you're part of the Body of Christ? Explain.

59.

WHAT IS COMMUNION?

Jesus took bread, blessed and broke it, and gave it to them and said, "Take, eat; this is My body."
MARK 14:22 NKJV

The night before He was betrayed, Jesus ate the Passover meal with His disciples. The Israelites had celebrated Passover every year since they'd been set free from slavery in Egypt, over a thousand years earlier. It was an important sign of the covenant between God and His people. But this night, Jesus infused the traditional meal with new meaning and used it to initiate a *new* covenant. Traditionally, each Jewish family sacrificed a Passover lamb on this day in remembrance of the fact that, long ago, the Angel of Death had "passed over" every house where the occupants had put the blood of the lamb on their doorposts.

Now Jesus Himself is the final, perfect Lamb of God, sacrificed for the sins of the world (John 1:29; 1 Peter 1:18–19). It is *His* blood that spares us from spiritual death. The Jews ate the lamb during the Passover meal, but this night Jesus took a loaf of bread, broke it, and said, "Take, eat; this is My body" (Mark 14:22 NKJV). Then He took a cup of wine and passed it around for them all to drink. He explained, "This is My blood of the new covenant" (Mark 14:24 NKJV). He instructed His followers to do this in memory of His death for their sins. Christians have celebrated the Lord's Supper (also called Communion) ever since.

At first it appears that Christians celebrated the Lord's Supper often, since "the breaking of bread" in Acts 2:42 likely refers to this meal. They probably did it every Sunday (Acts 20:7), and some denominations still do this. Most churches, however, feel that it gives more meaning to Communion if they don't celebrate it quite as often. But as Paul taught, *whenever* we eat of this bread and drink from this cup, we are proclaiming our faith in the Lord's sacrificial death (1 Corinthians 11:26).

DISCUSSION QUESTIONS

1. What made the Lord's Supper a *new* covenant?
2. How was Jesus the ultimate Passover lamb?
3. How often does your church celebrate Communion? Why?
4. How significant is the Lord's Supper to you?

60.

What Is Baptism, and Why Is It Important?

The baptism I'm talking about. . .promises God that you will keep a clear sense of what is right and wrong.
1 Peter 3:21 nirv

Baptism is a very important ceremony. The early Christians were usually baptized shortly after they believed in Jesus (Acts 2:41). Because Peter said, "Repent, and let every one of you be baptized in the name of Jesus Christ for the remission of sins" (Acts 2:38 nkjv), some Christian denominations teach that being baptized is *part* of salvation—that until persons are baptized, they're not yet saved. Baptism, they say, *completes* the process (Mark 16:16). If this teaching is correct, then baptism is critically important!

Most Christians—although they agree that baptism is important, and that every follower of Christ should be baptized—don't believe it's necessary for salvation. They believe that it is an outward sign of an inner change that has *already* happened. After all, the apostle Paul said, "Christ did not send me to baptize, but to preach the Gospel" (1 Corinthians 1:17 niv). If baptism was part of the Gospel, then Paul would have felt an urgent *need* to baptize new believers, because their salvation would not have been complete.

To be saved, you need to acknowledge that you're a sinner, repent of your sins, and put your faith in Jesus Christ to save you. Baptism, as 1 Peter 3:21 states, is a promise to God that you'll keep a clear sense of what is right and wrong. It is also a way to make a public commitment before other believers that, from this day forward, you'll follow Jesus faithfully. In addition, it's a way of identifying with Christ's death as we're "buried with Him through baptism" (Romans 6:4 NKJV). Then just as Christ was raised from the grave to eternal life, you come up out of the waters of baptism to live a new life as well. If you've never been baptized, plan to do it soon.

DISCUSSION QUESTIONS

1. Do you believe a person isn't saved until they're baptized? Why?
2. How is baptism an outward symbol of an inward change?
3. How is baptism a commitment and promise to God?
4. How is it also a public declaration to others?

61.

WHAT DOES IT MEAN TO BE FILLED WITH THE HOLY SPIRIT?

"But stay here in the city until the Holy Spirit comes and fills you with power from heaven."
LUKE 24:49 NLT

The apostle Paul advised Christians to "be filled with the Holy Spirit" (Ephesians 5:18 NIRV), but what does it mean to be *full* of the Spirit? And is it the same thing as being *baptized* with the Spirit? John the Baptist said, "I indeed baptized you with water, but He [Jesus] will baptize you with the Holy Spirit" (Mark 1:8 NKJV).

Many Christians believe that being baptized with the Holy Spirit means salvation—because the moment we accept Jesus as Lord, God sends the Spirit to live in our hearts (Galatians 4:6). Since all Christians *must* have the Spirit of Christ in their hearts to be saved (Romans 8:9), they believe that being baptized (or filled) with the Spirit means becoming a Christian.

Other Christians agree that the Holy Spirit "seals," or sets the mark of God's ownership, on believers when they're saved (Ephesians 1:13–14). But they insist that we receive only a *measure* of the Spirit to seal us and that being baptized with the Spirit is often a separate event. They point out that in the Bible, people sometimes received the Holy Spirit sometime *after* they became Christians (Acts 8:14–17; 19:1–6).

Still other Christians say that being "filled" with the Spirit is not a one-time event, but that God constantly pours out His Holy Spirit on those who *obey* Him (Acts 5:32). All Christians have the Holy Spirit, but when they obey God, He blesses them with even *more* of His Spirit. If they disobey God, His Spirit isn't present in as much power. That's why Paul urged those who were *already* Christians to be "filled" with the Holy Spirit.

DISCUSSION QUESTIONS

1. What do you believe "filled with the Spirit" means. Why?
2. Is this the same as the Baptism of the Spirit? Why or why not?
3. Do Spirit-filled Christians always *remain* full of the Spirit?

62.

WHAT IS THE FRUIT OF THE SPIRIT?

The fruit of the Spirit is love, joy, peace, forbearance, kindness, goodness, faithfulness, gentleness and self-control.
GALATIANS 5:22–23 NIV

Our outward attitude, words, and actions are our "fruit"—all of which are a reflection of who we are inside. For example, an apple tree, by virtue of the fact that it is an apple tree, bears apples. The natural fruit of a fig tree is figs. Jesus said that we could know the difference between a good and evil person by their fruit. We don't expect to gather grapes from thornbushes or figs from thistles. Even so, Jesus explained that every good tree bears good fruit, and every bad tree bears bad fruit (Matthew 7:15–20).

Our problem is that we are not consistently good. And no one but God is intrinsically good (Matthew 19:17). Humanity is fallen and our basic nature is sinful. We may try our best to *be* and *do* good, but we can't help but follow our natural, selfish inclinations much of the time. Paul calls this "the acts of the flesh" and lists several corrupt fruits: sexual immorality, impure thoughts and actions, hatred, jealousy, fits of rage, selfish ambition, envy, and drunkenness (Galatians 5:19–21). We don't always produce *all* the worst kinds of fruit—but we're often guilty of allowing it to bud in our hearts.

Fortunately for us, there is hope. Once we have the Holy Spirit living in our lives, the "fruit of the

Spirit" that appears is dramatically different from the fruit of our human nature. These good fruits—such as love, joy, peace, goodness, and self-control—are a natural outgrowth of the Holy Spirit and begin to appear once He's present in our lives. The Spirit also brings forth "purity, understanding, patience and kindness." (2 Corinthians 6:6 NIV). See also Ephesians 4:2; 5:9; and Colossians 3:12–15.

DISCUSSION QUESTIONS

1. What are some common "fruits" of selfish human nature?
2. What are the opposite *good* fruits of the Holy Spirit?
3. What fruit has the Spirit brought forth in *your* life?
4. How does a person grow *more* good fruit?

63.

Why Is It Important to Study the Bible?

"Think carefully about all of the words I have announced to you today. . . . They aren't just useless words for you. They are your very life."
Deuteronomy 32:46–47 NIrV

We can be lazy when it comes to studying God's Word. We often think that we learn *enough* Bible truths listening to sermons in church. True, we commend those who've read the Bible from cover to cover, and we admire people who spend time in daily Bible reading. But we ourselves are often too rushed in the morning or too tired after a long day's work to do so. Besides, isn't the basic message of the Bible "Love others and do good"? Don't we already *know* that?

Unfortunately, we can sometimes be ignorant of what the Bible says and *assume* that it teaches things it actually doesn't. For example, some Christians erroneously believe that the Bible says that all people are good and all religions are equally valid. But as Jesus said, "You are mistaken, because you do not know the Scriptures" (Matthew 22:29 NIrV). And while new Christians should be content with "the milk of the Word"—*basic* Bible truths—they must eventually grow up and eat solid food (1 Peter 2:2; Hebrews 5:13–14). If they don't, they'll stop growing spiritually.

Jesus promised, "The words I have spoken. . . are full of the Spirit and life" (John 6:63 NIV). He gave us His Word to help us in our time of need by encouraging us, breathing hope into our spirits, and engendering our trust in Him. If our hearts aren't full of God's Word, we more easily fall prey to discouragement and fear and don't have the spiritual strength we need to face life's challenges. Reading the Bible is not just something that "very devoted" Christians should do. *Every* Christian should study the Bible. It will require discipline to consistently make time for personal devotions, but the results are well worth the effort.

DISCUSSION QUESTIONS

1. How important is it to read and study the Bible?
2. How can ignorance of the scriptures be dangerous?
3. How does reading God's Word strengthen us?
4. How can you start a habit of daily Bible reading?

64.

WHY DO PEOPLE MEMORIZE BIBLE VERSES?

Your word I have hidden in my heart,
that I might not sin against You.
PSALM 119:11 NKJV

It's important to read God's Word so you know what it says and can differentiate between right and wrong. For that reason, it's also important to *remember* what you've read afterward. Some people remember passages of scripture because they love them so much and read them often. For example, they repeatedly find comfort when reading Psalm 23 or are constantly challenged when reading 1 Corinthians 13. They read these chapters so frequently that they've practically memorized them. So when they're discouraged or fearful, they think about Psalm 23 and are encouraged. Or when they're facing a difficult situation, they remember 1 Corinthians 13 and react in love. Or as Psalm 119:11 teaches, they avoid sin because they've hidden God's Word in their hearts and know what's right and wrong.

Some Christians take this one step further: they not only reread their favorite scriptures often but deliberately commit them to memory, repeating the verses over and over again until they know them by heart. Then they can carry their favorite chapter in their memory and quote it to themselves—silently or out loud—in times of need. Jesus also memorized key passages of the Bible, and during temptation, He was able to *quote* these verses to counter Satan's lies (Matthew 4:1–11).

Memorizing important verses also enables us to answer people's questions. God told the Israelites, "You shall lay up these words of mine in your heart and in your soul" (Deuteronomy 11:18 NKJV). Because they knew the scriptures by heart, they could teach them to their children and discuss them no matter *where* they were—in their house or walking down the road (1 Peter 3:15).

DISCUSSION QUESTIONS

1. Have you memorized any Bible verses? Which ones?
2. Which passages have you read so often that you practically memorized them?
3. Which chapters would you *like* to know by heart? Why?

65.

WHAT DOES THE BIBLE MEAN WHEN IT SAYS TO MEDITATE?

*Meditate on these things; give yourself entirely to them,
that your progress may be evident to all.*
1 TIMOTHY 4:15 NKJV

We shouldn't be surprised to learn that the Bible tells us to meditate. Meditation is an age-old principle taught in scripture, not merely something that Eastern religions teach. To meditate doesn't mean to let our minds go blank and think of absolutely nothing. We should be silent when we meditate, but biblical meditating means to ponder, to focus on, and to give deep and careful thought to something.

The first thing that we are to meditate on is the Lord Himself. King David said, "I meditate on You in the night watches" (Psalm 63:6 NKJV). Many people find that the night, when they've finished winding down from their day's activities and have quieted their spirit, is the ideal time for this. Isaac went out in the fields to meditate in the evening (Genesis 24:63).

We are not to think only of God—his awesome power, wisdom, and other attributes that *make* Him God—but we are also told to meditate on the miracles He has done. "I will. . .meditate on all your mighty deeds" (Psalm 77:12 NIV). When we remember that God has done great miracles in the past, and think deeply on the meaning of this, it inspires us to believe that He can do miracles for *us* in this modern day and age.

Lastly we are instructed to meditate on God's Word. David said that a righteous person delights in God's law, "and in His law he meditates day and night" (Psalm 1:2 NKJV). We are promised that if we do this, God will cause us to prosper and succeed (Joshua 1:8). This doesn't necessarily mean that we'll prosper financially—although it *can* mean that—but certainly we'll prosper spiritually.

DISCUSSION QUESTIONS

1. What is the biblical meaning of the word *meditate*?
2. What three things are we to meditate on?
3. How exactly can we meditate on God's Word "day and night"?
4. What benefits does God promise if we meditate?

66.

ARE CHRISTIANS SUPPOSED TO TITHE?

*Each of you should give what you have
decided in your heart to give.*
2 CORINTHIANS 9:7 NIV

Different churches have varying opinions about tithing. In Old Testament times, God commanded the Israelites to give 10 percent of all their earnings and flocks and crops to Him. "You must set aside a tithe of your crops—one-tenth of all the crops you harvest" (Deuteronomy 14:22 NLT). This tithe was used to support the Levites and priests, it was used for the upkeep of the temple, and it provided food for the poor and the widows and orphans. God promised to *bless* the Israelites if they tithed and warned that they'd be under a *curse* if they failed to (Malachi 3:8–12). Tithing was not an option.

Many churches believe that Christians today should *still* tithe. Although they agree that we're no longer under the law but under grace (Romans 6:14), they teach that the law regarding tithing remains in effect. In support of this, they point out that Jesus told the Pharisees that they were correct to tithe (Matthew 23:23). They also point out practical reasons: a tithing church has more finances and can do more to evangelize and help people. Since tithing is *still* a law of God, they believe that most financial problems are caused by Christians' failure to tithe.

Other churches believe that the old law is no

longer applicable (Galatians 3:24–25) and that the New Testament doesn't specifically instruct Christians to tithe. Instead, they're repeatedly told to give as much as they're able. Jesus talked a great deal about giving generously (Luke 6:38). And Paul also urged believers to cheerfully give as much as they felt they could—rather than giving out of a sense of obligation (2 Corinthians 9:6–8). Whether you believe in tithing or not, part of being a Christian is giving to God and others.

DISCUSSION QUESTIONS

1. Why is Malachi 3:8–12 often quoted to promote tithing?
2. Is the law concerning tithing still in effect? Why or why not?
3. If not, how much *are* Christians to give?
4. Why did Jesus talk so often about giving generously?

67.

How Can We Give Generously without Going Broke?

"Give, and you will receive. Your gift will return to you in full—pressed down, shaken together to make room for more, running over."

Luke 6:38 nlt

Churches who believe that members should tithe one-tenth of their income, teach that any "freewill offerings" they give——for building funds, missionaries, or alms for the poor——are *above and beyond* the 10 percent. Christians who give according to this principle are giving generously indeed! In fact, they're often giving sacrificially. Many would *like* to give that much, but a realistic look at their budget convinces them that they can't afford to.

If you believe in tithing, Malachi 3:10 states that *if* you tithe, God will open the floodgates of heaven and pour out such a blessing that there won't be room enough to receive it. Proverbs 3:9–10 echoes this thought. Even if you don't believe in tithing, but give generously and sacrificially, Jesus promised in Luke 6:38: "Give, and you will receive." Whatever you give will come back to you—and *then* some! Many Christians who've given to the Lord and others can testify that these principles work, and that God rewards those who give.

But bear in mind, God does *not* promise that *all* blessings you receive will be financial or material.

(Otherwise, "giving to God" would simply be one more materialistic investment plan with guaranteed dividends.) Often you're blessed in nonmaterial ways. As Jesus said, sometimes it is simply "more blessed to give than to receive" (Acts 20:35 NKJV). Other times the reward God gives will not be received in this life, but is a promise of "treasure in heaven" (Mark 10:21). God's desire is not for you to give *so* much that you're hard-pressed to pay your bills or provide for your own family (2 Corinthians 8:13; 1 Timothy 5:8). So give generously, yes, but give wisely.

DISCUSSION QUESTIONS

1. Has God ever blessed you financially for giving?
2. Have God's blessings to you *always* been financial or material?
3. How often is the main reward for giving "treasure in heaven"?
4. How can you give generously, yet wisely?

68.

What Are Spiritual Gifts?

Brothers and sisters, I want you to know
about the gifts of the Holy Spirit.
1 Corinthians 12:1 nirv

Each of us is born with various gifts and abilities, some are quite outstanding and others are more practical. We often call natural abilities "God-given gifts," especially if they're notable talents in music, art, or mathematics. But these are *not* the same as the gifts of the Holy Spirit, which are given to us *after* salvation. When the Holy Spirit enters our lives, He often gives us *new*, never-before-experienced abilities.

Paul states that although there are different gifts, each one is nevertheless given by the same Holy Spirit. In 1 Corinthians 12:8–10, he lists some gifts: wisdom, knowledge, faith, gifts of healing, power to do miracles, prophecy, tongues, and the ability to interpret tongues. Many Christians believe that all these gifts are *still* in use in the Church today. Others believe that they *were* used in a special way to usher in the Christian Church in its beginning but are no longer necessary.

While the gifts of tongues and prophecy are frequently questioned, it's difficult to deny that God's Spirit still gives believers gifts of wisdom, knowledge, and faith. And the *purpose* of these gifts is beyond dispute. Many people who are *naturally* wise or who have knowledge are prone to pride, feeling that their abilities make them special. They often use their abilities to draw attention to themselves. But the gifts of the Holy Spirit are given so that we can *minister* to other Christians. They are given "for the good of all" (1 Corinthians 12:7 NIrv).

If you think that you haven't received a spiritual gift yet, ask God to give you one. Look closely at your life and the way God *already* uses you to help others. Even the desire to be helpful and encourage others can be a gift of the Spirit.

DISCUSSION QUESTIONS

1. Why does God give Christians "gifts of the Spirit"?
2. Why does God give each of us *different* gifts?
3. Are all the gifts in Paul's list still given to believers today?
4. What spiritual gift has God given you?

69.

WHAT IS SPIRITUAL WARFARE?

*The weapons of our warfare are not carnal but mighty in
God for pulling down strongholds.*
2 CORINTHIANS 10:4 NKJV

We know that the devil and his demons exist and that
they oppose God's will. It should come as no surprise
then to learn that there are sometimes fierce, pitched
battles in the heavens. On one occasion, the archangel
Michael led the armies of heaven in open war against
the devil and his angels (Revelation 12:7). We're not
exempt from this warfare, since Satan opposes God's
will in *our* lives and seeks to hinder answers to *our*
prayers. Our foes are unseen but very real. As Paul
states in Ephesians 6:12, we don't battle against flesh-
and-blood enemies, but against evil powers, against the
wicked rulers of spiritual darkness.

Whether we *seek* this battle or not, it sometimes
comes to us. That's why we're to be ready at *all* times,
because we never know when the "day of evil" will
come. We're advised to "put on the full armor of God,"
so that when we're under spiritual attack, we may be
able to stand our ground and not become a casualty
(Ephesians 6:13 NIV). (For a full description of what
the armor of God consists of, read Ephesians 6:10–
18.) The *good* news is that Jesus Christ in our hearts is
greater than all the forces of the enemy (1 John 4:4),
and we're promised that if we steadfastly resist the
devil, he *will* flee from us (James 4:7).

Spiritual warfare also involves *us* attacking Satan's strongholds. We do this through prayer—often by prayer and fasting. Paul wrote to the early Christians, "Join in my struggle by praying to God for me" (Romans 15:30 NLT). We shouldn't just pray for victory over the enemy's attacks on *our* lives; we should pray for our fellow Christians as well (Matthew 12:28–29).

DISCUSSION QUESTIONS

1. What do you think "spiritual warfare" means?
2. Have you ever felt like you were under spiritual attack? Describe it.
3. What did you *do* to win the battle? Was it easy?
4. What comforting promises does the Bible give us?

70.

How Should We Worship God?

*"God is Spirit, and those who worship Him
must worship in spirit and truth."*
John 4:24 NKJV

Christians worship God in a number of different ways. More traditional churches often sing time-honored hymns accompanied by a piano or organ. Worship is quiet, reverent, and orderly. Worship in more contemporary churches, however, is often quite a bit more lively and consists of exuberant singing, loud modern instruments, spontaneous outbursts of praise, and believers clapping and raising their hands. The worship in most churches falls between these two examples. While each congregation finds their own manifestations important, the most *vital* thing is that Christians are sincerely worshipping God.

Despite the great variety in the way we worship, we still have many things in common. Though we can praise God alone in the midst of nature, silently in our hearts, all churches believe that the Bible *also* calls us to united, vocal worship. As David said, "Praise God in the great congregation" (Psalm 68:26 NIV). Also, music and singing have always been an important part of God's worship: "I will sing the Lord's praise" (Psalm 13:6 NIV). And while there is certainly a time for solemn, meaningful hymns, Christians have a great deal to be *happy* about, and there are occasions when we are to worship the Lord with gladness and sing joyful songs to Him (Psalm 100:2). Some churches even believe that the Bible's instructions to "shout for joy" still apply today (Psalm 33:1–3).

Bowing down and humbly kneeling before God, whether privately or in public, has always been a part of His worship (Psalm 95:6). The ancient Jews didn't hesitate to raise their hands while praying (Psalm 134:2). These expressions of worship are still important to many churches, and less so to others, but the important thing is that we're sincerely focused on worshipping God.

DISCUSSION QUESTIONS

1. What is the most important thing about worshipping God?
2. Which expressions of worship mean a lot to *you*?
3. Is loud worship more sincere than quiet worship?
4. Can *any* form of worship become mere ritual? How?

71.

HOW CAN I FIGURE OUT WHAT GOD'S WILL IS?

Seek his will in all you do, and he will show you which path to take.
PROVERBS 3:6 NLT

The most important step in discovering God's will is to sincerely *desire* His will. This may seem obvious, but by nature people seek security and comfort—and try to avoid insecurity and hardships. So often when we're seeking *God's* will, we're actually presenting our *own* desires to Him and seeking His approval. Even Jesus acknowledged that He wanted to avoid dying on the cross—although He knew it was His Father's will. That's why He prayed, "Not My will, but Yours, be done" (Luke 22:42 NKJV). While God has promised to give us "whatever we ask" in prayer, this is *only* if we're focused on doing what pleases Him (1 John 3:22).

Proverbs 3:6 says that if we seek God's will in *all* we do, He will show us which path to choose. This proverb has two important facets. First, it's easier to find God's will in uncertain, complex situations if we're already consistently following His will in obvious everyday choices. Much of the time, we *know* what God wants; we know what's right because we've read it in His Word (Romans 2:18). If we're already in the habit of obeying God, when we face a new situation, we'll more easily recognize what we should do.

And second, "seeking God's will" also means

praying for Him to direct us. Seeking God's will sometimes means having the wisdom to choose between various options. If we're not set on our own desires but are open to what *God* wants in our lives, we're more apt to make the right choice. Like Jesus, we must sincerely seek the will of the Father (John 5:30). God may give us the desires of our heart, or He may require us to surrender them.

DISCUSSION QUESTIONS

1. What is the first step in discovering God's will?
2. Which habits make finding God's will easier?
3. Read God's promise in 1 John 3:22. What do you think?

72.

Can I Actually Hear God Speak?

*"When the Spirit of truth comes,
he will guide you into all truth."*
John 16:13 NLT

Yes, God speaks to *all* Christians. After all, the Bible is His Word, and when we read it, we're hearing God speak to us. "All Scripture is. . .useful for teaching, rebuking, correcting and training in righteousness" (2 Timothy 3:16 NIV). Jesus also promised His disciples that the Holy Spirit would teach them *all* things—and He mostly did this by reminding them of what Jesus had already said (John 14:26). Fortunately, the disciples left us a written record so *we* can benefit from Christ's words, too. But only the Holy Spirit can *truly* open our eyes to what we're reading (Psalm 119:18). That's why it's important to pray, "Lord, speak to me through Your Word."

Christians also believe that God makes His directions obvious to them by changing their circumstances and making their course of action obvious when they ask Him for direction. In addition, many Christians believe that God speaks to them by impressing on their hearts that they *should* or should *not* do something. And still other Christians believe that God sometimes speaks to them in "a still small voice" (1 Kings 19:12 KJV). They don't claim that these are audible words—simply that a message impresses itself upon their mind.

Some Christians take this a step further and

believe that God's promise to the early Church—that He would pour out His Spirit on them and they would prophesy—is still valid today (Acts 2:17). Other Christians advise caution and point out that it's easy to speak from our own imagination and assume that we're hearing from God (Jeremiah 23:21). In fact, in *whatever* way we believe that God is speaking to us, we're wise to make sure that it lines up with scripture. We also do well to seek a second opinion from pastors and godly mentors (Proverbs 11:14).

DISCUSSION QUESTIONS

1. Have you ever felt a Bible verse speak *directly* to you?
2. How does God usually speak to you?
3. Has God ever spoken to you in a *new* way? How?
4. Have you ever mistakenly thought you heard from God?

73.

What Does It Mean to "Witness" to Others?

Always be prepared to give an answer to everyone who asks you to give the reason for the hope that you have.
1 Peter 3:15 niv

To *witness* something means to see and hear it with your own eyes and ears. Later when you tell others about what happened, you're witnessing. You are testifying just like witnesses in court case give their testimony. When speaking about Jesus being alive again from the dead, Peter said, "We are all witnesses of this" (Acts 2:32 nlt). Now none of us were alive two thousand years ago when Jesus was resurrected. However, we *can* testify about how we've found the Bible's teachings to be true and how Jesus has changed our lives. This is called "giving our testimony."

In a larger sense, sharing the Gospel—the Good News about Jesus Christ—is called witnessing. Jesus told His disciples, "Go into all the world and preach the gospel" (Mark 16:15 nkjv), and they did. Jesus' command didn't apply just to them. *All* Christians should be witnesses for Jesus. And it's important that we do this not just with our *words*, but with our *lifestyles*. Jesus told us to live in such a way that people would see our good works and glorify God as a result (Matthew 5:16). Then when they ask why we live the way we do and why we believe what we believe, we should be ready to give them an answer.

But many of us are hesitant to speak to others about Jesus. We either don't want to be thought of as "religious" or "preachy" or we're concerned about offending someone. In some cases, we're actually ashamed to speak about the Lord. The best cure for this is for us to ask God to fill us with His Holy Spirit, because it's God's Spirit who gives us the power to speak out boldly for Jesus (Acts 1:8).

DISCUSSION QUESTIONS

1. What does "to witness" mean?
2. What does it mean to "give our testimony"?
3. Have you shared the Gospel with anyone? What was the result?
4. How can we overcome hesitation and fear about witnessing?

74.

ARE CHRISTIANS EXPECTED TO RESIST ALL TEMPTATION?

"Watch and pray so that you will not fall into temptation."
MATTHEW 26:41 NIV

God knows that we have weaknesses, and He knows that we're vulnerable to temptation in those areas. As David pointed out, the Lord remembers that we are but dust, and He has pity on those who fear Him, just as a father pities His children (Psalm 103:13–14). God knows that we're often weak. But this is not an excuse to blatantly give in to temptation and then say, "God will forgive me." He forgives those who fall in a moment of weakness and sudden temptation, but stumbling is quite different from planning ahead of time to jump feet first into sin.

Jesus stated that "the flesh is weak," but this statement of fact was not to excuse moral failure. Rather, He used the opportunity to give His disciples the solution: "Watch and pray, lest you enter into temptation" (Mark 14:38 NKJV). Yes, the flesh is weak, but God can strengthen us if we pray. If we're aware of our weaknesses and "watch," we're far less likely to be ambushed by sin. If our primary desire is to please God, we'll give compromising situations a wide berth. Many ex-alcoholics, for example, completely avoid any place where they might be exposed to even the *sight* or *smell* of alcohol. Those with a weakness for pornography know they must keep control of their hearts and eyes at *all* times. "Do not give the devil a foothold" (Ephesians 4:27 NIV).

We can't avoid all temptation, but just the same, we don't have to surrender. God doesn't abandon us in a moment of testing. If we're praying for the will-power to obey Him, He'll be sure not to let the sinful desire overwhelm us. He'll make a way for us to escape its clutches (1 Corinthians 10:13). This might mean physically *fleeing* the scene of temptation.

DISCUSSION QUESTIONS

1. Do you know anyone who resists *all* temptation? Who?
2. How can the fear of God help us resist temptation?
3. How effective have you found Jesus' advice to "watch and pray"?
4. Why is it good to *avoid* being tempted if you can?

75.

WHY IS IT IMPORTANT TO FORGIVE OTHERS?

"But if you do not forgive others their sins,
your Father will not forgive your sins."
MATTHEW 6:15 NIV

There are several reasons why we should forgive others when they offend or hurt us. One of the most important ones is that God is love. He loves all people, and if we're His children and His Holy Spirit dwells in our hearts, we'll love them as well. In fact, He made it a commandment: the person who loves God *must* love others (1 John 4:20–21). Solomon said that whoever overlooks a wrong does so because they *love* the person who wronged them (Proverbs 17:9), but it's difficult to love someone while refusing to forgive them.

We also need to bear in mind that God forgave us all *our* sins when we accepted Christ's punishment on the cross in our place. And in turn He asks that we forgive. The Bible tells to "forgive each other, just as God forgave you" (Ephesians 4:32 NIRV). Jesus warned that if we *don't* forgive others, God is under no obligation to forgive us *our* sins (Matthew 18:35). Why is He so strict on this point? Because to refuse to forgive is to refuse the power of forgiveness. To forgive releases the love and power of God in our lives and liberates us from bitterness. It's to our own benefit to forgive.

But forgiving is not always easy. Often the offenses that we hang on to are petty and *should* be quickly forgiven. But God understands that when we've been maliciously hurt by someone, forgiveness may not be easy. He understands that it may take time. It will certainly take prayer and yielding our will to God's—and it will often cause us tears. But if we ask God for more of His Holy Spirit and ask Him to *help* us forgive, He will do it.

DISCUSSION QUESTIONS

1. How is forgiveness an evidence of love?
2. Why is it so important for us to forgive others?
3. How is forgiveness liberating and healing for us personally?
4. Is forgiveness always easy? Why or why not?

Scripture Index